JUMP START

A NORTHWEST
RENAISSANCE ANTHOLOGY

Compiled by
Northwest Renaissance Poets

2009

ISBN: 978-0-9743264-8-1

Cover and book design: C. L. Knight
Cover photograph: ©iStockphoto.com/Martti Salmela

Steel Toe Books
Department of English
Western Kentucky University
1906 College Heights Blvd., #11086
Bowling Green, KY 42101-1086
www.steeltoebooks.com

History of the Jump Start Workshops

The Jump Start Your Writing series began with a conversation between Lonny Kaneko and Susan Landgraf. Both teach at Highline Community College and are board members of The Northwest Renaissance, a non-profit literary and performing arts organization with a thirty-year history. They proposed a partnership with the college through the Center of Extended Learning to offer poetry workshops led by a different poet or artist each month.

The series began with poet Muriel Nelson in October 2000 and finished with poet Susan Landgraf in May 2006. Workshops for community writers, as well as Highline students, staff, and faculty, were held once a month in October and November, and January through May. Each featured a lecture or presentation, sometimes with video and audio, and writing in response to exercises. Participants were encouraged to share their work (most enthusiastically did so), and some wonderful pieces came out of those workshops. Some highlights were postcard poems taught by Washington State's first Poet Laureate Sam Green, cut-and-paste visual poetry introduced by Arlene Naganawa, chapbooks presented by Ann Spiers, and comics and poetry taught by Craig McKenney.

The series was organized by Susan Landgraf, and she and Sharon Hashimoto hosted the seven years of workshops.

This collection shows the breadth and depth of the thirty-four participating poets and artists. Thanks to all the writers and participants for fine works created during the Jump Start Your Writing series.

Workshop Leaders

October, 2000	Muriel Nelson
November, 2000	Susan Landgraf
January, 2001	Lonny Kaneko
February, 2001	Deborah Bacharach
March, 2001	Paul Nelson
April, 2001	Marjorie Rommel
October, 2001	Sharon Hashimoto
November, 2001	Allen Braden
January, 2002	Susan Landgraf
February, 2002	Susan Rich
March, 2002	Ann Spiers
April, 2002	Kevin Miller
May, 2002	Penny Gerking
October, 2002	Susan Landgraf
November, 2002	Elizabeth Austen
January, 2003	Donna Frisk
February, 2003	Sam Green
March, 2003	Robert Hasselblad and Maria Groat
April, 2003	Alice Derry
May, 2003	Arlene Naganawa
October, 2003	Marjorie Rommel
November, 2003	Muriel Nelson
January, 2004	Pesha Gertler
February, 2004	Diane Westergaard
March, 2004	Susan Rich
April, 2004	Kevin Miller
May, 2004	Joe Green
October 7, 2004	Peter Pereira
October 28, 2004	Holly Hughes
November, 2004	Christopher Jarmick
January, 2005	Jill McGrath
February, 2005	Allison Green
March, 2005	Janée Baugher
April, 2005	Tatyana Mishel
May, 2005	Marjorie Manwaring
October, 2005	Paul Nelson
November, 2005	Anne Sweet
February, 2006	Craig McKenney
March, 2006	Sati Mookherjee
April, 2006	Phyllis Collier
May, 2006	Susan Landgraf

Contents

JUMP
START

On Punctuation

not for me the dogma of the period
preaching order and a sure conclusion
and no not for me the prissy
formality or tight-lipped fence
of the colon and as for the semi-
colon call it what it is
a period slumming
with the commas
a poseur at the bar
feigning liberation with one hand
tightening the leash with the other
oh give me the headlong run-on
fragment dangling its feet
over the edge give me the sly
comma with its come-hither
wave teasing all the characters
on either side give me
ellipses (not just a gang of periods)
a trail of possibilities
or give me the sweet interrupting dash
the running leaping joining dash all the voices
gleeing out over one another
oh if I must
punctuate
give me the YIPPEE
of the exclamation point
give me give me the curling
cupping curve mounting the period
with voluptuous uncertainty

Seattle Review

In Praise of Orality
an infant manifesto

only love the world wetly
lean in, lick the nearest anything
bathe it in sweet spit, the delicious
suck of discovery

oh mouth, oh omnivorous organ!
oh edible world!

soon, soon we meet by sight
arm's length, in words—
leaving more and more
world untasted

2003 Jack Straw Writers Anthology
Weathered Pages: The Poetry Pole

This Morning

Light takes the Tree; but who can tell us how?
—Roethke

It's time. It's almost too late.
Did you see the magnolia light its pink fires?
You could be your own, unknown self.
No one is keeping it from you.

The magnolia lights its pink fires
daffodils shed papery sheaths.
No one is keeping you from it—
your church of window, pen and morning.

Daffodils undress, shed papery sheaths—
gestures invisible to the eye.
In the church of window, pen and morning
what unfolds at frequencies we can't see?

Gestures invisible to naked eye,
the garden opens, an untranslatable book
written at a frequency we can't see.
Not a psalm, exactly, but a segue.

The garden opens, an untranslatable book.
You can be your own unknown self—
not a psalm, but a segue.
It's time.

Pontoon 7

3

Man Who Built a Life-Size Crucifix from Toothpicks

1.

Spent his working years
with a jackhammer.
Never thought he'd find himself
with tweezers and smooth slivers
of wood. One glue drop
at a time, nudging toothpicks
into a heel, an arch. Scared
him how easy they'd snap.

Years he labored on the hair.
Sometimes he wanted
to burn the whole thing
down. When the rib cage
wouldn't hold, when he had to learn
the slope between fingers, the height
of knuckles, every line that cuts
through the palm. He's just a man.
He wasn't put on this earth
to cure the sick or throw a fastball.
But if there has to be a crown,
he has to make it.

2.

He's a church-going man; his wife
can live with that. He likes to see her
dressed up, pretty in the pew.
She'd sit on the garage floor with
the boxes and boxes of toothpicks.
Who's making you do this? she'd ask.

He finished the damn thing.
Put it in the yard and rigged lights.
People flocked to their house like
it was an Elvis sighting.
Once she drove by. There Jesus was
on the cross. There he was in a
lawn chair, calm as glass, gazing up
with a love they had never had.

At Thirteen

The waistband of my gym shorts
folded over by the abundance of soft flesh.
Glasses smudged with sweat.
Quick in the classroom,
silent, stumbling in the gym.

When the other girls discuss
black, no, purple eyeliner,
I refuse to comment.
Vapid, I think, vain.
Watch disdainfully as they clamp
their lashes in metal vises.

But at night, in front of my mirror,
I drape a black Turkish scarf
around my overflowing curves,
roll my hips like a temptress.
Smear vasoline on my eyelids,
layer on sparkles from the craftbox.
Heavy under squares of gold,
with each over-the-shoulder-side-long look,
my eyes outshine my braces.

South Coast Poetry Journal

After We Fight

In my dream, 4:00 a.m. is bright red
and the New York street grid
shifts. I balance a yellow block.
If I move, all is lost. My choice:
stick to home or dangle.
Either way, love is an abstraction.

bovine free Wyoming!

Is Not

— after the painting "Woman Resting, Dreaming"
by Jason Bourguignon (b. 1970)

I. At the Studio

One 60-watt bulb on me and one to cast the canvas yellow.
This dank atelier smells of oils—titanium white, cobalt blue.
Overhead, a 757's decisive flight pattern.

Behind the studio, a train's mechanical clank,
then the guttural call of engineer to caboose.
Oh to hop that train, to quit this stiff pose and his hundred eyes.

While he paints in a smock spotted with crimson,
sometimes it's just the heater's hum we hear.
I imagine him with a bowl of pears instead of me as he says:

> *Look, pears, for months this is how I saw it…*
> *You changed color on me, but never objected,*
> *never slept, never suggested Bach. Now*
> *part of you I'll eat, part of you I'll toss.*
> *This painting is all that will remain.*

Here in this studio, havocked with stacks of canvases,
objects for still-lifes and exposed brick.

II. The Model

You don't see the blue beneath skin,
how it wishes to unmask itself in sea.
You don't sense the stain on her cheek,
how a single hand could strike it.
You don't hear two people silent,
and you don't know their breaths.
Yes, there were two of them:
as she lay skin-sprawled
he stood summoning shapes.

Some things he hid in painting her.

III. The Painting

Notice the studio floor's purple?
Actually, the floor was a worn white.
Notice the pillow?
There was no pillow.
See, he worked without allegiance.
He merely painted what he knew:
months in a warehouse in Georgetown
where trains glide to the east
while stockyard metal shears above.
Now the picture is done.
Not once did he touch her.
Her Everywoman face
and body's serpentine outline,
one arm wrenched over the head
and each limb caught at its joint.
A dab of sienna for the umbilicus,
this model's nexus to all that is Mother
and all that is lost.

Each portrait is part right, part wrong.
Blood gives flesh life, this much is true.

At Juniper-Berries Lake
in Montagny-Les-Beaune France, I Consider Travel

This morning, a young boy bikes to the opposite shore.
He casts his line. And waits.

     Water breezes west.
     Birds, strident in the oak trees.
     Clouds meander east.

He reels in nothing. He climbs on his bike
and goes back the way he came.

     The wet line drips
     as he holds both pole and handlebars.
     Bicycle wheels: steadfast over pebbly earth.

The chain's slow, insistent squeak
trails him home.

Inspiration

Not far from where a coyote leads you
over the sparsely timbered hillside,
you find a feather held in the sagebrush
flanking an abandoned logging road.
You know the pattern, its bars of tan
almost the color of parchment
or more like that coyote's pelt actually.
The feather of a great barred owl.
You could say the darker, narrower
scribbles curving in toward the quill
suggest a line of silhouettes in flight.
You could say a lesson might exist
in the wind's subtle dispersal of dust
trickling through Sheepskull Gap,
estranging that feather from its wing.
All you really need to tell anyone
is how a single feather is poised
so the tip of the quill writes on thin air.

Dense Growth

Hubbard's Falcon

Though these words are most likely
For a peregrine, I cannot help feeling
Drawn to names such as kestrel or merlin

For a heightening of intentional lyric,
An attempt to adorn, or moderate even,
The notions of which men are capable.

By men I suppose that I mean you
Or myself, members of a people governed
By the same irrepressibility which led

Our grandfathers to stone certain birds
And split them open to study the way
The future was coiled inside their flesh.

But what possible good can come of this,
One of us spoiling for some prized target,
The rarity of forcing a bird of prey down?

What good, a falconer might as well ask
When he finally stumbles upon his bird,
The unhooded light gone from its eyes,

Camouflaged but for a red flag of blood
Spreading underneath the lodgepole pine.
There is no question that he must abandon

All of what remains where the feathers
And drying blood grow indistinguishable
Already from the needles and earth,

His task now being that of any survivor:
To tally the lost, to print or chisel names
Across the malleable tablets of memory.

Remember this: with falconry or elegy,
Instructions are conveyed for our mutual good
On how to release and ascend from the self

Then a striking and rending in open space
And the inevitable returning with a burden,
A grief to swallow and fuel the living body.

Seneca Review and *Poets at the Canterbury Faire*

Premonition

I have to tell you about the barn owls
caught every year between our silos
in a hopper for grain pulverized into flour.
Before dying they squeezed in through a vent
that would have been screened up
except for the old man's unspoken want
of laying his hands on something beautiful
or wild, of swiping a fistful of wing feathers
and selecting the best one for his Stetson.
At night his child remembers what comes next:
the bird nailed by dead wings to a hewn joist
or strung up feet-first above the salt lick,
the bucket of bone meal, the rat poison.
Its expression in rigor mortis pinched up
like someone taking a drag from a cigarette,
the face convulsive as if ready to cry out.

Witness

Hermione

At nine, I could barely reach part way
Around her flowery hips and thighs.
I longed for the sun on her skin,
To squeeze from her all she held—
Her years, the secrets of her mystical birth
Before she would abandon me
For the god of a far-off battlefield.

Again I asked, *Was I born from you?*
Or hatched from an egg like they said?
I was no swan,
But the blue Easter chick in the yard
Who took me for its mother.

Before what terror waited
I held tight to the tattered rabbit
Frozen in photograph.
I try to break through the firewall,
Drone of warplanes on their way,
Once more to reach around her,
Lose myself again in the print
Of her housedress.

Deo Gratias

You knew I would find this place,
That one day I would be
Ready to stand quiet

Before such gift, to listen
For each breath of the mesquite.
To hear all the tamarisk has to say.

You made this desert look as if
Nothing much ever happens. It was
For me to find the color of sand,

The largo movement of pre-Cambrian rock.
Yucca brevifolia lifts its arms. Time sees
Through every guise, strips me to bone,

Does not make an easy peace,
But waits to present itself in the right light.
These were your promises:

In the heat of late afternoon, I am
Washed clean. When I leave,
This desert will go with me.

A Certain Hunger

A knobby finger of mainland
Marks the beginning of the end of a journey
To find out how far north we dare go
Where life is passed in nautical miles.

We drop anchor in the ale of August,
Nights of shoreline riddled with rocks.
Find ways to make the loons laugh—
Torpedo range on yesterday's chart,

Ketchikan's narrow throat at midnight,
A mooring where fathoms lower from 20 to 1
While we aren't looking. We could wish
For a red-roofed store with coolers of bait,

Float plane to airlift us out. Or we could love
What waits far enough to be called lost,
Places the isobath charts don't show,
Where there is always another reef or current.

Phosphorescence disappears with the tide
That brings us back forever changed.
Coast Mountains lean on us to leave
What is not ours—steep-to channels

Leading to light, grizzlies on the bank.
In a deceiving stillness we look back
To depths sufficient to drag us down
To where no one would ever know.

Rosewater/Grandmother

The scent of rosewater, sweet as liqueur, takes me
back to grandmother's bedroom where lotions in jars
multiply in the vanity mirror. I see

a tortoise-shell comb and brush laid out like jewels
on a glass tray. Hairpins spill from a china bowl;
the aroma of roses gluts the air and jags

my memory. Tall and all-knowing, she told
me to brush my hair a hundred strokes a night.
For keen eyes and curly hair, she sold

me on eating carrots. She said I'd never need
to pluck my eyebrows; I didn't really trust her.
Forty years later, my son who never knew

her, sends me a bottle of Kiehl's French Rosewater.
It stings my eyes and crowds the room, grandmother.

Seattle Review

The Gift

He quietly shoves the apple into my hand
and disappears. My face flushes red.
I meander home from school, slipping past
                              prim Cape Cods

with aging clapboards. The windows blink. I measure
crisp, waxy flesh: it's the biggest Delicious
I've ever seen—a five-pointed treasure.
                              I open our door

and avoid my mother's eyes. Upstairs, I flop
on my bed and hold the fruit to the light. It shines
like a precious gem. At night, I hide it on top
                              of the dresser, behind

a Storybook doll called Rose Red. A couple of weeks
filter by; he wants to know if I liked it.
I cross my fingers and tell him, "It was neat."
                              How can I

admit it's rotting in my room? Where
are words to say it was too perfect a gift—
that the hard cider smell perfumes the air
                              and reminds me of him?

Poetry Seattle and *Tablets the Rain Inscribes*

Bird Babies

I see myself as a child: robins who own
the apple tree wake me each morning at five.
They chatter and hoot, darting outside my window.

I drift back into darkness. The squealing cry
of a bluejay nags me awake. It's no jay:
it's the blasted baby again. I'm twenty-nine

with six kids under seven. Plotting escape,
I burrow under blankets; the child won't
let me alone. I drag out drugged and shake

another bottle. The scene fades; the show
moves on. I wake as pink blossoms scratch
against my window. Now it's now; I know

bird babies nest in the tree. I watch
as tiny beaks scissor the air for the catch.

The Written Arts

Hardhack in Bloom,

and the palomino comes right up to the gate.

Along Old Olympic highway
fireweed rises
in one measured stand after the next.

That should be enough color to get started.

When Piotr Anderszewski,
the Ukranian who now lives in Paris,
played in Chicago a month ago,
we were supposed to think he *was* Chopin.

OK. I go along willingly
back to the scene I've kept from *Masterpiece Theater*,
glass doors opening to Majorcan sunshine,
palms, and islands of languid flowers.

Sand—and you get the feeling he might have called her George—

lounges on the sofa while he plays,
this the fiery decade of their affair,
the last of his life,

consumed from inside and out,
she, as ravenous for his music as I am,

the only thing I listen to the week my mother-in-law
lies in the hospital,
her tests gradually bringing
the shadowy mass of the first scan
to lymphoma.

It's all that helps,
music which tramples,
which seizes,
which takes me between its jaws
and doesn't let go.
Huge, rolling chords of the romantics—
"Those strange, ground-breaking, left hand chords,"
the critic writes, "chromaticism...which pierces
the heart."

While his right hand rills like creek water
over stones.

Or gallops the limits of a fenced field.

Two decades already ticked by
since Keats had blazed forth
and was gone,
TB as unequivocal in the words
as bloom.

I still want to be Sand, daring
and in the most impossible love,
slouched against the door frame,
while Chopin, as he disappears, plays to me,
and late afternoon gives way.

Debt, her children, his Poland.
They breathe
in the mild air and music.

"My heart aches," Keats begins his "Ode to a Nightingale,"
bold and direct.

"Now more than ever it seems rich to die,"
but he talks himself out of it by the end of the poem.

"Darkling I listen" and he means in the northern summer dusk
which never seems to let go.

I tell you, when the hardhack's in bloom
and trefoil's weedy yellow has splashed up the road embankments
overwhelming the wild daisies,

when blackberries are on
and the Himalayas begin their month-long
cycle from pink muslin to green knots to
what's going to be juice in our mouths,
all the while mounted on the most terrific barbs,

so we loiter in the sun
picking our fingers stained,
and in the ditches the patches of simple heal-all
blazon purple and true,

then summer most generous,
most warm,
Keats on his way to Italy,
knowing all the time he was leaving warmth,
he was leaving Fanny.

Connected

It's a day
for stoking the wood stove,
for sorting through boxes and files
while the wind
blows song sparrows off course,
while blackcapped chickadees
think twice about making
their skittish flights
from the Hawthorne tree
to easy food at the feeder.

I prepare lunch—
a flowered bowl brimming
with tomato soup,
crusty bread spread
with soft butter,
lemon-ginger tea in a glass mug
steeping to pale yellow.
On my table the bounty
of the world.

The gray wind outside
gnashing at crisp leaves,
the soft quiet inside
wrapping me like feathers,
fire sucking up the flue—
such a day. A day
with no errands,
no have-to-do projects
poking like a burr.
A day, though half gone,
holding all the possibility
of primordial ooze.

Enter the Bell Jar

A flash of red sizzles like fire
in late afternoon sun
as it pulls its head back
again and again to listen for ants,
the rhythmic rap unmistakable.
Shadows close fast around us,
yet we stand as in a bell jar
with this master of deconstruction
who flings bark on our heads.
Though wisdom tells us to get
down the trail before night wraps us
entirely in black, we can't move.

Native Americans believed
the woodpecker a good omen.
Has it come to follow,
or to lead?   Suddenly
its pterodactyl-like cry
stutters on air and it's gone.
But the brand of its spirit burns.

Of Glistening Mica

She's nearly 30 before she makes
her first long distance drive alone.
She packs the blue VW
then heads west from Portland
out the Sunset Highway,
veering left to Vernonia
and the Oregon coast.

The turning of the trees,
the silver sentinels
of the Tillamook Burn,
the glistening Wilson River
pouring wildly
out of the coast range,
more exhilarating
than when filtered
through the scrim
of parent, boyfriend, husband—
the revelation that even alone,
especially alone,
she can tap into the mysteries
trapped in the intelligence
of roadside weeds.

She walks the beach, rolling
to that peculiar longing
the pounding surf stirs
in the human heart,
an unnamed pulsing
pushing toward light and life
to make itself known as joy.

She skips unfettered
over myriad scatterings
of mica stars.

Father

He was a rooster of a man, proudly shrill,
dominating his flock with noise and spurs.
He was an ass of a man, braying, untiring, bearing
a load twice his size by dint of stubborn will.
He was a god of a man, handsome, capricious, careless
where he scattered his golden seed, his sudden scorn.
He was a monkey of a man, scratching at himself,
clowning, grabbing, peering out through sad, wise, primate eyes.
He was a magpie of a man, raucous, rapacious, daring,
harbinger of trouble, necessary but unloved.
He was a bear of a man, bowling my life before him,
his impatient sweat shaping my days, his brown hands feeding me.

Green Tricycle

Anniversary

Our love is a stone,
granite heavy, between us,
bruising my hip where I carry it,
pushing you away.

It shrinks and lightens,
mica seams sparkling,
silver specks refracting light.

It lays itself down as marble,
dark-veined and solemn,
beneath our feet. Under
our pillows it curves warmly,

smooth vermilion river rock.
Inside our shoes it travels,
a grey poppy-seed pebble,
constant reminder, raising blisters,

but always our stone, our rock, our marble,
our lucky piece in every pocket.

In Love's Name

*In memory of Caden, Dimitri, Eli, LaTosha,
and all those children whose names
have been forgotten*

He loved him, he said,
red-faced and weeping, he loved him
like his own son. He wouldn't hurt him,
he cried, hands to the sky,
he loved him.

He loved him, she said, shocked and pale.
He would never do that, he loved him.

Like his own son he loved him,
while he stroked the back, the ribs,
the legs, those thin rods, thick rope,
narrow wire, used with loving care.

She loved him, forgetting to feed him,
shutting the door on his midnight sobs,
it pained her to hear him cry, always
crying, she loved him too much to listen.

His love was so forceful, sitting
on the belly, swinging him by the head,
pushing the small face beneath water.

She loved him, had a picture of him,
in his hand-me-down clothes, bare feet, burned hands,
his sad and tremulous smile.

At last, they simply loved him to death.

And still she loves him, arms open to him as he
is taken from the courtroom, tears streaming
as he passes without a glance, but oh
> *she loves him,*
>> *loves him,*
>>> *loves him.*

Red River Review

The Mermaids and the Seated Women

I
We sit, in rows,
street upon street,
very still, like wood
in our wooden chairs
in our matching houses and gowns,
our long hair pulled back,
we stare straight ahead.
To our left, the mermaids,
their laughter and song
rounding the sea air.

II
Once in the full tide
of our dreaming, a mermaid
appeared, pouring a potion of liquid
pearl, while we drank the gleaming white
fluid, she sang of the luminous depths
in ourselves. A scattering
of silver and she was gone, leaving
a shiver of salt
on our skin and the courage
to almost lift our long skirts
and see if we too had tails.

III
Today one of the chairs
is empty. Turning, we see her, awash
in a surf of glistening arms
and fins, wafting, rippling on the swell, loose
hair billowing
on the wind, their silvery
voices calling. All night
we hear them, calling, a trembling
of lights from the deep
that shimmers, undulates
in our spines. Tomorrow, in the hush
of ebb tide,
another chair will be empty.

Poetry Northwest

The Center of the Hora

In August I danced
the hora barefoot on the gold
spangled grass I danced the last hora
while still you lived
leaping barefoot in my long red dress
leaping while the Klezmers
sang in the green air: Noladeth Le Shalom
I danced o Papa I danced
in that golden moment
while still you lived
though you lay dying
I danced my love for you
barefoot on the gold
spangled grass while
you lived I danced
while still it was possible for God
to say yes instead of no
while one of us might have
been intelligent enough or loving enough
or magical enough to lure you back
you of the golden heart of mandolins

and music and magic you who danced
on the streets as I danced on the grass
while still you lived

and everything was possible
And still I am there Papa
part of me dancing in winter
on summer grass
dancing in a circle
around the shining skull
at the center of the hora

dancing to your alive face
until at last you sway with me
and we dance o how we dance
while death shines beneath our feet

Jewish Women's Literary Annual 2001

Annual Medical Exam

How smugly we hold onto
our temporary lives;
all accidents, all dyings happen
to the Other
though we toss on nights
before our annual exam
and chatter nervously when the needle
pokes our skin, our blood tested
to see if we pass or fail.
Walking from the parking lot,
we smoke (if we smoke) heartily,
puffing what may be our last
free act before the hospital owns us.
All the tests return negative.
We pass. More life. Tomorrow,
we'll take up jogging. The loan
is good for another year.

Crosscurrents

Letter to Saharla

Dear Saharla,

I am giving you a C- on your essay. I am sorry. You are writing about an experience that was obviously very traumatic for you, and it is difficult for me to attach a letter grade to that experience. However, that was what I was hired to do.

The English Department has decided that essays that don't meet a minimum level of competency on all standards must automatically be given a C- or below. Your essay has a pattern of verb tense and subject-verb agreement errors. The minimum level of competency in grammar requires an ability to manage verb tenses and subject-verb agreement. You can see, then, that a C- is my only option. In fact, a C- is the most generous of all the options available to me.

Other faculty members—outside the English Department, mostly—are very concerned about the grade average on our campus. The average grade on our campus is a B-, which they think is too high. They think a better average grade would be a C. I find it very difficult to give a C, or, as in your case, a C-. A C seems very low to me, and I think about what it must feel to receive it. I have never received a C in my life. The lowest grade I ever received was a B. It was for driver's ed, in high school.

However, rest assured that the other parts of your essay are meeting minimal standards. Your essay has a clear thesis, stated at the end of your introduction. The introduction grabs the reader's attention (it grabbed my attention). Your transitions could be stronger, but I am not confused by the essay's organization. The best thing about the essay is its vivid and engaging detail. When you describe the way the soldiers came into your house and killed your parents in front of you and your sister, I feel as if I am right there.

I am sure you will be able to manage verb tense and subject-verb agreement in the future, perhaps by the end of the quarter. Try not to let the C- bother you.

Words for the New Hire

The names on your roster
are not your neighbors' names.
Before you go in there, practice:
Katarina, Halima, Nguyen.

You'll need to lasso their adjectives,
sulking behind nouns. Spit articles at their pages.
They'll be accountants,

                    not poets.

Don't let them tell their stories:
by boat or by foot, the dead fathers
they didn't bury, the mothers
they didn't know. They wrote those stories
last term. We've read those stories

                          before.

Treat them the same. Thu misses class
to interpret; Andrey must have got through
high school with his smile. If you give Thu more
time, Andrey will want more. If you give
Andrey more time....

Vary your assignments; they're prone
to copying. Quiz them on the details; they're prone
to skimming. Keep them apart;
they'll talk about

                you.

You didn't vote for the president
who made that war. No one asked you
what to do with
        them.

ZYZZYVA

Conjugations

Verde que te quiero verde.
    — Federico García Lorca

Verde que te quiero verde.
In the car, steamed windows—the headlights
on for hours—you recited verde
que te quiero verde. Over oysters, sun
on the Sound, you poured wine
from your glass into mine, and I didn't know
you were saying green how you loved me
green. Eventually the battery
must be jumped, the car started. Eventually
I am practicing my conjugations: quiero, quieres,
quiere. Under white down you read aloud
and meaning slivers through—a word,
a phrase has come to mean the thing
it represents. Queremos, queréis, quieren.
My tongue pedals behind my teeth;
when you say bésame, my mouth hears
only your desire. This falling
into language is like falling in love—
the anxieties of vocab, the satisfactions
of agreement. Sometimes, though, in present
tense I miss the freefall of those kisses in the car—
no preterite, no imperfect future. I miss
the sound of Spanish in your mouth
when it meant only sound—
verde que te quiero verde—and it thrummed
meaningless and meaning full
against my heart.

The Jealous Gods

When He made the Big Bang
the rest of us told Him how splendid it was,
but we really meant it could have been bigger,

could have tossed its particles farther,
ought to have made a much louder sound.
We meant it didn't look like much so far,

just a lot of little sparkles in the infinite dark.
So He said it wasn't even finished yet.
He said it was still expanding and anyway

He was the one who had gone to all the trouble
of putting it together, so we might as well
shove off. Which is pretty much what we did.

Naturally, we had to use the rest of our floods first,
and thunderbolts and swarming clouds of locusts,
but every single time we did, it was a disaster;

nothing truly epochal ever happened.
Then, eventually, the calendar caught up with us,
and after that our days were numbered.

ZYZZYVA

Little Finger

*Like most women her age, she traditionally cuts off
a finger each time a relative or close friend dies.*
— Phil Borges, from the caption to his
Portrait of Enalia, 50, Jiowika, Irian Jaya.

I was the first to go,
the runt of the left hand
litter, smallest of the lot,
but not necessarily the least
important or weakest.

I was her booger hooker,
her eye-corner cleaner,
the wax extractor
for her left ear.
I picked out secrets

that I would never tell.
You might have known me
anywhere by my nail,
my hook, my crooked
knuckle, before I fell.

But who can say how the living
will survive? I remember how,
wringing a chicken's neck, I felt it give.
I was a pioneer. I was the first to go.
I know what it means to be lonely.

Free Lunch
The epigraph is taken from *Enduring Spirit* by Phil Borges
and is used by permission of Phil Borges Studio, Inc.,
and Bridges to Understanding.

One Dog Barking

My neighbor's dog is busy
sending messages, barking
three times, pausing

as if he's listening,
then barking three times again.
Perhaps he is calling someone who is not at home.

Or maybe he is signaling space alien dogs,
broadcasting his own ancient name—*Wolf!*
Wolf! Wolf! —and waiting

for them to answer. This may take a while,
but he is patient. He has been at it, repeating
the same thing, doggedly, all night.

Poetry Motel/ Wallpaper Broadside Series;
Dogs Cats Crows: A Black Heron Press Animal Anthology

Bearing the Word

You could try holding a ripe quail's egg
in your teeth & jogging across broken
ground until you can do this without cracking
the shell; you could try wrapping your tongue
in tar-soaked gauze, & chanting spells
you somehow know might heal
if only you could say them
cleanly; try gathering the shards of Anisazi
pots from the tops of a dozen Arizona mesas
& then begin the work of assembling a single one
from all those parts until it will hold
water; do this blindfolded.
        Nothing, nothing
can prepare you to carry the words
that tell your wife that her sweet, beloved
mother, is dying. There is nothing but the daily
practice of being full as a barrel
catching rain from a clean roof,
to which she can come as her own
terrible thirst requires.

The Grace of Necessity

Some Reasons Why I Became a Poet

Because I wanted to undo each stitch
in time, unravel the nine seams
that inhibit remembering; because I wanted
to roll a stone with such tenderness
that moss would grow & hold light
on all sides at once; because I wanted to teach
every old dog I saw a new set of tricks;
because I wanted to lead a blind horse
to water & make her believe her thirst
mattered; because I wanted to count
the chickens of grief & gain before they hatched;
because I never wanted to let sleeping cats lie
in wait beneath the birdbath; because
I wanted to close the barn door after the last
horse went grazing & know that something
important was left stalled inside; because
I wanted to welcome all Greeks & the desperate
bearing of their gifts; & because I couldn't stop
keeping my poor mouth open in a sort
of continual awe, trusting that flies, like
words, would come & go in their own good time.

The Grace of Necessity

Old Man Folding a Kerchief in the Supermarket

for Hayden Carruth

He has used it to wipe the filth
from the table where his daughter
has left him to do her shopping
spilling it from the pocket of his jacket
like a small blue lake
the color of an old house dress.

Now he is folding it back into shape
with blunt fingers, hunched
over his labor, watching intently
his hands as though
they might betray him.

For ten minutes this has been
his whole work, & he has gathered
all the deliberate threads
of his attention into this single
act, oblivious to the fact
that anyone might be watching,
that he might be teaching us all
how to live.

The Grace of Necessity

Sciurus Griseus

We hear a clatter, a rattle
of toes scrambling the bark
of a hazel wood tree. Then the pitch
of shells striking the deck. I charge

the sliding glass door, rapping
my knuckles and yelling through
the screen. When I turn my back,
they're nibbling my budding nasturtiums,

the gray flags of their tails twitching
a code for dinner. I grit my teeth,
forgetting the time when I scattered
acorns like a farmer casting seeds

from a shoulder-slung bag or the grooves
they gnawed in the wooden box,
frozen shut with snow and twenty degrees—
the smell of peanuts permeating

the air. Just out of reach, they pause
to scratch fleas from their fur, chitter
their animal laugh, and dance from foot
to foot. When I lunge for the door,

they're already running. Their weight seesaws
the limb, bending it like a bow to shoot
gray blurs through the trees, arms and legs
spread as if to grab the arc of their flight.

Seattle Woman

What My Blind Grandfather Showed Me

His big hands outstretched,
I believed those fingers could reshape shadows,
his open palms push away the night
as he reached for the chair's back,
the blunt blade of a table. Everything
was softer in moonlight. I didn't see
his eyes, only the tilt of his head
when he listened to the rug
brush against his bare feet.
Knowing I watched him, did he feel
my breath's thin release? Slowly, I let him
guide me over walls and edges, the cool handles
of the buffet. Exposed in the morning's harsh light,
I stood in a room surrounded by his touch.

Asian Pacific American Journal

In Hawaii, We Do This

No one wanted to
hold my hand at Brighton Elementary
when the wart appeared at the base
of my ring finger. It was lumpy with ridges
like the barnacles speckling
ocean stones. I wore bow-tied dresses
with pockets, keeping my fist closed.
And under pressure, in the damp heat
of my fingers, the wart dug in and grew.

The doctor's glowing punk
couldn't burn hot or deep enough. Maybe Dad
saw that I believed more in frog spit
and the harsh words of my friends.
In Hawaii, my father said, *we do this*
and his knife split the eggplant. Two tear shapes
fell to the sides. Dad rubbed the juice
into my hand. Then I followed him
to the far corner of our backyard
where the day seemed dim. No one
would believe me, I thought, as we buried
the eggplant. I smelled the earth
as Dad's shovel tamped it down. He nodded
with the rhythm of his words: *When this rots,*
your wart will die and fall off. All the way
back in to dinner, he held my sticky hand.

Pontoon 14

Superman's Last Date

Lois lit the fire
in her kitchen,
watched it engulf
stove, cabinets.
Then she gathered the basics:
      lipstick
      flask of gin
      the jam-jar
and moved to wait at the window
over the butcher shop.

Later, over candle light
and a shimmer of rare meat,
the wine red and full
as her questions,
he made it clear.

"We have to stop
repeating this ritual.
I am bound to save you,
whether from tornado or flood,
car crash or pool of blood—
but these weekly fires—"

He sighed, the S expanding
on his blue chest
like an old snake, too tired
even to talk to the woman.

It was then she slipped
the jam-jar of kryptonite
from her purse.

The night crew
found him crumpled
beneath the karaoke machine,
one rose placed
between his teeth.

StringTown

Word Salad

The poem offers its lure.
Applications are available
at point of pen moving,
swish of syllables
as they parade
across the axis
of harnessed dream.

Verbs may be asked
to work extra hours.
Peruse, plead,
laugh, litigate, loot,
inflate, flush, fling,
hyper-ventilate.
Do try to keep up.

Nouns will be given
badges, clean uniforms.
Blank stare, mustard,
marble, blind date,
data, long division,
free will, fire code.
You know the drill.

Articles will be tested
for individual honesty.
Finalists will form
a phalanx of dust particles
beneath the head table.
Short answers
will be rewarded.

Conjunctions likewise
either or also plus minus
neither therefore insofar
since however and
notwithstanding –
until tongues tangle
in the service of sound.

The poem rises
like a chimera
from longitudinal studies,
and dances with the rain
against lazy hours,
light bulbs bare
against old ego.

Visual Verse in collaboration with textile artist Maria Groat

Subplot

When the first words leave
the flesh of my tongue
and enter the thin bone
of your inner ear,
the Olympic Mountains align
along a seismographer's spine
to form villanelles.

And later, after the opera
of rock and ice fades
into twilight's blind eye,
death comes up to us
wearing a red cape,
offers to let us live
up to her expectations.

In this subplot, we learn
to walk backwards
across old fairy tales
into the wolf's throat.
To circle the fire,
the growling that feeds us
one to the other.

Visual Verse in collaboration with textile artist Maria Groat

Robert Hasselblad and Maria Groat in Collaboration

Word Salad 1 (detail)

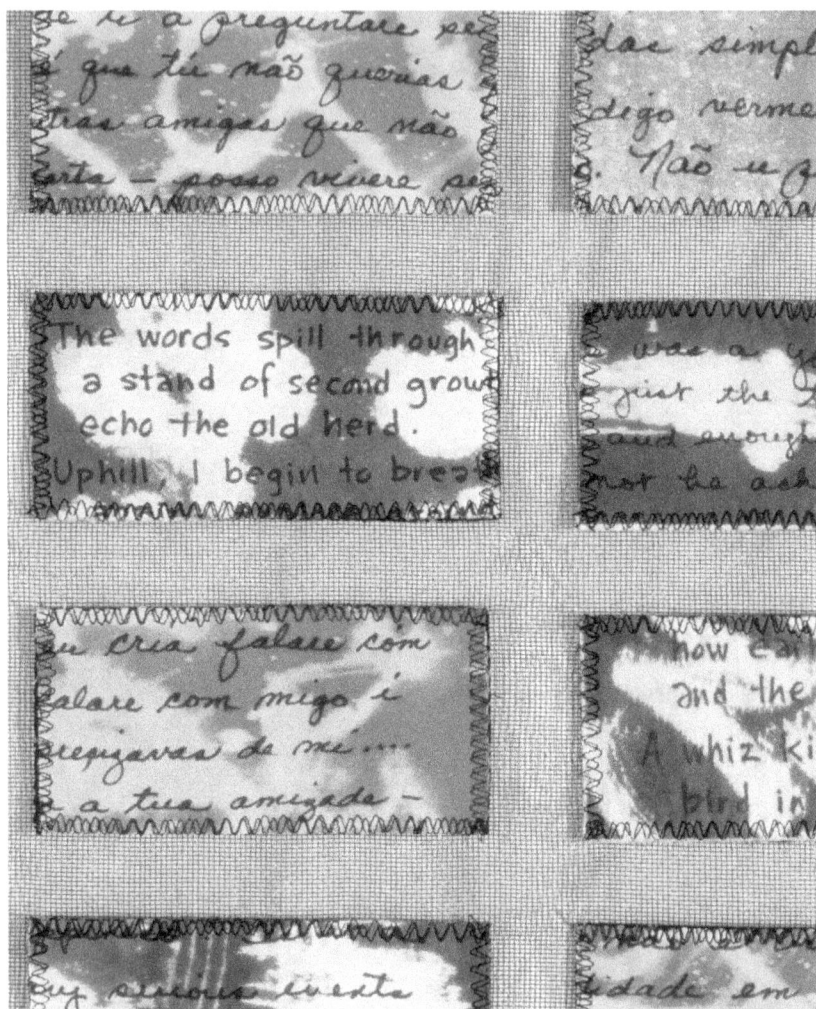

Word Salad Too (detail)

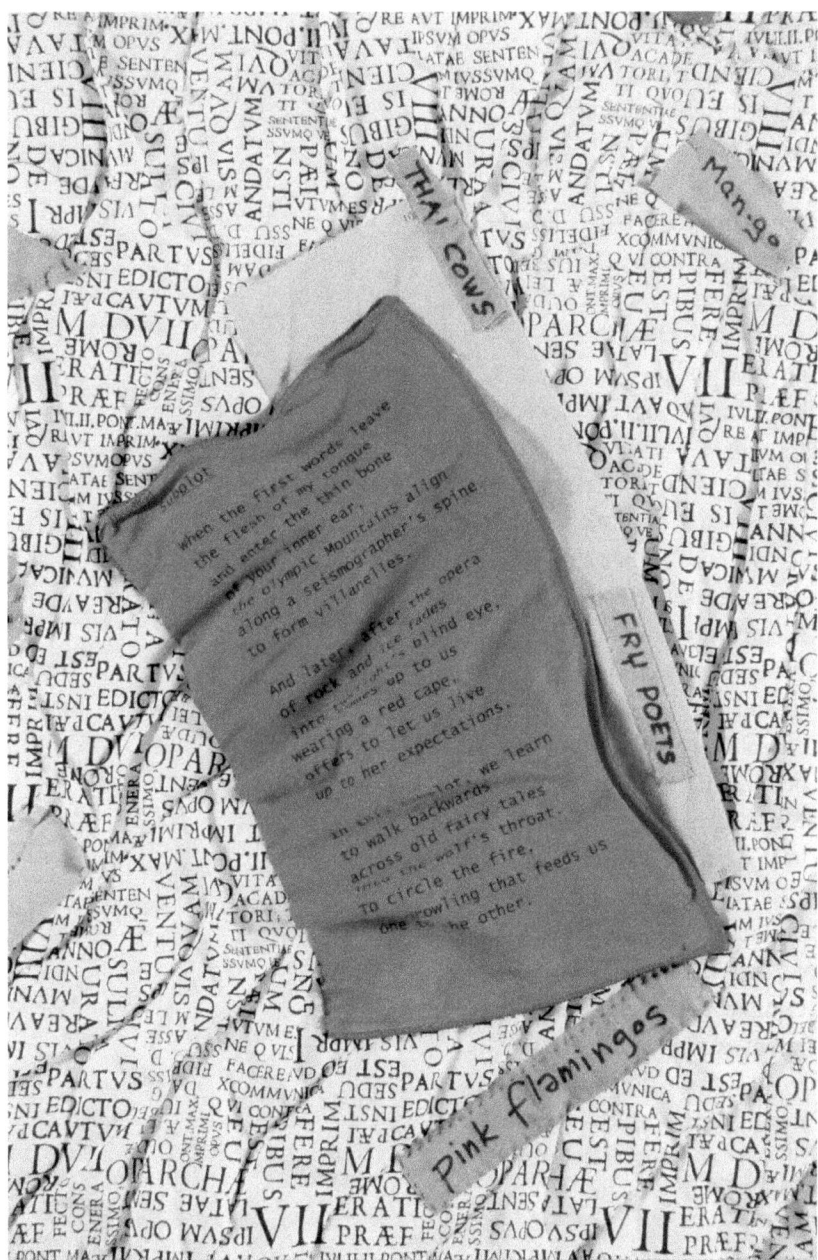

The Bath

The tub fills inch by inch,
as I kneel beside it, trail my fingers
in the bright braid of water.
Mom perches on the toilet seat,
entranced by the ritual until
she realizes the bath's for her.
Oh no, she says, drawing her
three layers of shirts to her chest,
crossing her arms and legs.
Oh no, I couldn't, she repeats,
brow furrowing, that look I now
recognize like an approaching squall.
I abandon reason, the hygiene argument,
promise a Hershey's bar, if she will just,
please, take off her clothes. *Oh no,*
she repeats, her voice rising.
Meanwhile, the water is cooling.
I strip off my clothes, step into it,
let the warm water take me
completely, slipping down until
only my face shines up, a moon mask.
Mom stays with me, interested now
in this turn of events. I sit up.
Will you wash my back, Mom?
So much gone, but let this
still be there. She bends over
to dip the washcloth in the still
warm water, squeezes it,
lets it dribble down my back,
leans over to rub the butter pat
of soap, swiping each armpit,

then rinses off the suds with long
practiced strokes. I turn around
to thank her, catch her smiling,
lips pursed, humming,
still a mother with a daughter
whose back needs washing.

Alaska Quarterly Review, Pontoon 8

What Daughters Do

Peaches arrived each July in their purple nests
of tissue, fine jewels inside the wood-slatted crate.
One by one, we'd uncover them, still warm from the sun,

lay the soft fuzz against our cheek, press gently, testing readiness.
Our job: slicing them for pies, what daughters do,
while mom mixed flour and Crisco for the crust.

I never learned to make pie crust from her. When, finally I asked,
it was too late. She stared, puzzled, at the rolling pin,
handed it back to me, said, *Here honey, you do it.*

Now I am learning to make pie crust, remembering all I saw.
My tanned hands roll out the crust in full moons, draw it thinner,
more translucent with each stroke, fold it neatly into quarters, slip it

onto the pie plate, unfold the quarters like wings, then crimp
the crust, thumb nestling between the fingers in small arcs
until the crust ripples, circling, more continuous

than memory, claiming its hands.

Poet as Art Reading Series broadside by Egress Studios

The Mammogram

She's done this a few times before, it's clear
by the detached way she takes my left breast,
lifts it like a soft pear onto the cold plate,
scrunches it until it's aligned
with the small etched mountain-like
elevations on a topo map, cross sections
of breasts, all sizes, the democracy
of the mammogram. We are all equal
before this machine, obedient
like children. So, I try not
to grimace as the machine bears down,
flattens my breast like dough
under a rolling pin, distract myself
by describing the odd shape:
ear of cat, triangular hat, fin of orca.
I even hold my breath before I am told.
She lifts the bruised pear off the plate,
cups the next one in her objective hands,
lines it up, rolling the flesh into place.
I wonder: *does she think they are too small?*
How much easier her job with breasts
she can corral, spill onto the glass,
no doubt, then, significant flesh is
wedged between the plates. Instead,
she tries to draw more flesh in,
stroking my armpit, pressing me closer
to the steel table. My breasts, tender
white doves, want to spring this
cage of metal and glass, but they huddle
before the machine, quiescent,
as it hums and clicks four times,
twice on each side and I matter-of-factly
lift each arm to waltz with my cold partner.

I wonder how many breasts have been here?
Fifty a day, she tells me, half smile escaping,
as she checks the film. *A card in the mail,*
she says, *if nothing shows up. Otherwise,*
we'll call you, voice flat, distant again.
I return to my car, pay $3 for parking,
merge back into traffic and my life,
this shared humiliation, our century's
rite for women, awaiting that call,
rolling the dice, knowing the odds are
one in seven it will be me
and if not me, someone I love,
someone I love.

Kalliope

Musives and a Silent Crump

Musive was a fine word, the name of a moth, gone extinct.
Crump: the sound of a heavy shell or bomb. *Hurkle*: a crouching,
cowering motion. *Erump*: to erupt, burst forth. Were these words
phased out, slow, or did they surface and then disappear,
shy as whale backs? Maybe they entered and exited the language
in a rush, like *groovy*, *rad*, and *word up*, slang terms teens use,
then don't use, like hangouts turned "wack"
by the sudden arrival of parents. So many words,
but none for the smiles that flickered from Jane to me,

and back, when we'd reached a place in our life together
where we almost didn't need words. No word for
the strange joy I felt, cutting our firstborn son's umbilical cord
as he lay screaming on Jane's stomach. So many words,
but none tickled our infant son's throat.
Jane and I came to understand, this cry meant *I'm hungry*,
that one meant *burp me*, another meant *change me*.
Italians have seven words for "the," so why can't we
have words that distinguish a baby's different types of tears,

or a special word for the tears on Jane's face as she dug
her fingernails into her cheeks after he died in his crib?
Have you ever scratched someone, by accident,
as your arms grazed? I know the word for that. It's *scrazing*,
but I had no words to comfort Jane. *I'm sorry. It'll be okay.*
I knew these words didn't mean as much as I needed them to.
I had no words for the beasts eating my insides, musives
in a trunk full of clothes, no words for the hole I felt
and tried to fill with my writing, with my music,

with Camels and Jim Beam. And when Jane sought comfort
in another man's arms, when I found a red strand
of that man's hair on my pillow, on my bed,

when I was forced to imagine their wordless moans,
a silent crump shocked my senses, left me hurkling, unable to erump.
The words *cuckold* and *how could you?* and *I'll kill him!*
weren't there for me. *Wife* and *son* had turned into archaisms.
I had nothing but my dictionary, which grunted, sighed, and shrugged,
a friend who had no words that could comfort me.

TriQuarterly

The Spirits Say "Stay Away"

We are the shadows around your car
and every building you've ever driven past.
We are broke and broken, no triggers
to squeeze, no gas pedals to gun.
We've been evicted from our homes
made of bones. You say you can't go on

because you miss some Miss
who has averted her blue eyes
that sparkle like they've seen
Jesus, Mary, and the Seven Wonders.
You've visited our neighborhood twice before:
once when you carved

a cross in your wrist and watched
your life start spilling out;
a second time when you sighed and wrapped
your lips around the barrel of your handgun,
but not before we opened our mouths
and suctioned the bullets out.

We became guns ourselves
and spat rounds into each other.
What of it? We were already dead.
You unroll the windows
on your chipped-red Mustang,
close the garage door. The gas fumes

enter you, turn you into a race car,
hellbent on the finish line.
We're going to siphon your gas
and mess with your radio dial

until your sad song changes
to something cheery.

Ah music, we used to live for that.

Poems & Plays

Ecstasy

At eighteen, when Frieda Lowe and I
split a heavy dose of impure X at a party,
Frieda lifted her knees to her chest
and wrapped them in her arms, as if
her ribs needed a second cage to keep
her heart from flying away.

Love, I think I'm hallucinating
when I watch our firstborn belly-surf
on a rainbow-shaped pillow
as I rock his baby brother to sleep.

Leaving the party, Frieda and I parted for
good. She tripped down a cliff.
 Hospital. Stomach pump. I
broke down and directed traffic, after a
lady cop, at the end of her shift, handed me
some flares, and said good luck.

I'm flashing back to a night when
raindrops crashed on the roof of this
home we part own, part owe on. A sliver
of moonlight through the curtain
showed me your naked body.

The flares streaked across the sky like bolt lightning.
I waved them in all directions and believed in God
racing through my bloodstream. I kept
believing until I fell down hard, got caught.
Psych ward. County detox. Rehab. Jail.
Forty days and nights inside the flood.

When lightning bit the sky that night,
rain stopped falling all at once,
replaced by the moans of crickets.
Our bodies coming together were
a song of hope the moonlight sang to the darkness.

The Texas Review

I Hate Peggy Lee

I hate Peggy Lee.
I hate her for that song she did.
You know the one.
The one where she talks through most of it
and then sings
'If that's all there is
then let's keep dancin'.
Let's break out the booze
and have a ball.'
in a voice that tells you she's lived too much,
seen too much,
backed up with that damn banjo;
happy banjo, sad strings, old voice.

It's a great song, one of the best
Jerry Leiber and Mike Stoller ever wrote
but I wish 'em horrible deaths
for creating that cursed thing.

You start thinking about what you done with your life
and whether it seems like you done a lot
or you done nothin' at all, you think,
... is that all there is?

You decide to get smarter about these things,
it don't do you any good thinking about things like that—
just depresses you, brings you down
and there's already plenty of things
to be down about
without letting someone else's tuneful lament
suck the false optimism out of you.

So you turn it off, don't think about it
never play the song and just pretend
it never existed.

It's a fine strategy and it works for a while
but then you'll hear someone say the phrase,
or you'll hear the song on a radio,
or on a jukebox,

or someone walks by you whistling the tune—
not your fault—
but it's back in your head again.

You're watching a really good TV show,
or a movie everyone calls a classic,
or you read a great book
and as you get to the end
you say,
that was pretty good
but. . .

Screw it,
so what,
who said there has to be more.
You're okay with it, again ...

But,
not really.
You can not escape it.
You see some sports player make a spectacular play,
an Olympic athlete makes a new world's record,
you have the most incredible sexual experience of your life,
or you just laughed so hard it made your eyes water.

You can be feeling as low as any man ever felt
or be feeling so good you wonder how it will
ever get any better,
and then you hear it.
Right before you go to sleep
or when you're standing,
just standin'
watching a spectacular sunset
with a double rainbow,
sunbeams breaking
through cotton ball clouds,
shimmerin' off some
tranquil azure blue
body of water ...

I hate Peggy Lee.

Another Flirtation

Her words were suspended

like seeds in a package
at the hardware store.

She waited too long to respond,
and the smile—

oh, it was a nice enough smile—

wasn't enough.

Things that See through You

1
Santa Claus runs his fingers through your hair and asks,
"Are you a good boy?" He will search what lurks
in your heart. No matter what you answer, he says,
"Speak only the truth your shadow knows."

2
Your doctor asks if you've been exercising
and you tell him that you work out every day
by walking to class and you practice meditation
by standing in front of your students, breathing evenly
when they stare blankly and have no answers.
When he hears these words, he merely stares at you.

3
The man who sees through walls, iron vaults, bedroom doors
saves victims from the pestilence of foul play. When Lois looks at him,
she sees steel, but when he looks at her, does he see
the beauty of her face and breasts or evil cells
that will chase her down the alleys of her life?

4
CT scans the body and beeps like a robot saying
all is well today; tomorrow brings another set of troubles.
The big circle circles your body, winks and inches
toward the feet, all the while looking for the weakness
that is you in the density of your bones.

5
A sensitive wife always knows when a female student
sits in your office day after day, asking questions
like what do I need to take to major in American

literature? She knows when you take the long way home
over the Green River bridge or through Algona.

6
When you are five your mother
knows when you fail to clean your room,
put your dolls on the shelf, unhook the train cars
and unplug the transformer or change your underwear.
Your mother hears of your demise before you do.

7
The future is a blank wall you can't see through.
It's a wool blanket or an opening door.
What you can't see when you open your eyes you see
in the dark waiting for morning light.

Wild Light

We stand before the long building
others call "latrine," my father and I,
in the dark, looking where stars
should shine but where storm clouds roll
on themselves as they do in time-lapse
photography. Rain strikes like little nails;
a jagged torch catches a still photograph:
our faces upturned to catch the rain
catch the light. The smell of it erases
the new lumber of our room, the dirt
and plaster, the new urine on new concrete.
In seconds thunder echoes back. Again
and again, lightning follows lightning.
Each flash rips the Idaho sky as we struggle
through dust or snow or rain to pee.

Like folding chairs, we've been installed
in unfinished rooms. My parents have
carried me through the upheaval of rifles,
baggage tags, catcalls and the daily journeys
of the mind into semi-arid flats,
until this electric moment. Midnight,
and the child's mind rises. The yellow balloon
they have carried me in pops like thunder.
My father's hand wilts in mine. I am alone
in the storm's passage, dispossessed of bed
and apple trees. Each toy, each dust wisp,
each tricycle track that charts my universe
is shattered by the sharp squeal
of light, the last bark of thunder.

That's when light, like a wild hare,
darting through sage, in a rattle-
struck leap, lifts itself free
of the damp sack of land. In the eye
of light is a will sky-wide and deep
as darkness. My leap, brief as the hole
lightning makes in the sky, is free
of barbed wire and any brimstone cup
of words. I am pursued by the mystery
that rushes nameless across the desert
after its own blinding imagination.

Seattle Review

Bailey Gatzert: The First Grade, 1945

Miss Riley stands above me, fading fast
beneath the porcelain light that frames her face.
Her finger, raised to God, declares each word,
each careful pencil mark must fill the void
between the faded lines. She measures us
the way she measures words like *brother, house,*
like *sister, sky* and *dog.* The way she measured
Stanley by standing him against the chalkboard.

The words are always only hers. She draws
the list and keeps the rules. The sky is bruised
but never green, a house can be magenta
and sister pink but never yellow. She matches
objects to their hues. We learn her world,
but she is never part of ours. She would
never walk down alleys, never visit
one room homes too poor to invite a guest,

or running water, a stove, or ice. She hawks
us in the class. No boy dares laugh or talk.
An easel slants its errant legs as if
to trip the unaware; we tiptoe past it.
(Three long snows, a gift from Franklin D.,
has taught us how, without apology,
to live behind barbed wire and journey home.)
We learned to quiet trembling mouths and hands.

Words contain our thought. They tell just who
we really are, or camouflage the fool,
the quiet stranger who lies behind the smile.
One day, I whisper, "Benjo….Benjo." I try
to tell her what I mean. "What did you say?"

Her question rocks the room and laughter sails
on wings about my ears. She checks her list.
No *benjo* there. "O-benjo!" I can't lose

control: frustration pools a cadmium stain
across the floor. Miss Riley turns, her silence
a naked finger: Enemy! I've mixed
American and Japanese. She rakes
her memory—does she hear the dying cries
of boys who toppled easels, erased the sky,
then grew to manhood on the way to war?
My hand's raised to heaven. I'm here. I'm here.

An Ear to the Ground

Gathering Cockles, Willapa Bay, Oysterville

Addictive, Dan the Oyster Man, said.
You have to set yourself a limit. Imagine
what it was like for the first whites, cockles
for the taking and oysters, clams, quail, deer, duck.

Size of a child's fist, cockles marked like tree rings, variegated
ivory and black tumbled in the channel, some submerged
in the sand, nuggets scooped and dropped
in the holey buckets, and the nursery rhyme stuck
like a seed in my teeth: cockles crying *cockles…alive, alive o.*

We cut through the fast-running, sun-glinted water
with our hands. Dan talked over the the wind. *Chinooks*
and Quinaults who were here died off with measles
and smallpox and the oyster beds died

soon after with growing demand from around
the country, oysters shipped in ice to San Francisco
where they went well with cigars and scotch,
and Oysterville boomed with taverns and churches.
Up the road the cemetery grew headstones,

Indian and white alike. Blackberries grew faster
than spades could cover the graves. Thunder Bird,
who made men, was there; God the father
and Christ were there; and Toolux, the south wind.

Okay, just a half bucket more, three blue plastic bags full,
the bay quiet except for the wind and then popping
sounds like little hands clapping—zing, zing—silver
perch strafing our legs, thighs, outstretched hands, the fish
flipping in and out of the long green grass like a mesh net

over the channel, over the oyster beds, the mussels
and cockles crying *cockles...alive, alive o*
and Toolux, always Toolux crying,
I am the south wind.

Nimrod

The Would-be Namibian Doctor Speaks

Wherever you look, there is healing
to be done.

Water holes have dried. Tribes
have been separated. Bushmen make
arrows from the quiver trees
but few hunt. They eat porridge.

A crab spider catches a fly
on the Welwitschia, some of the plants
old as Christ. Tourists tear off strips.
They walk on the Baobab roots
in their hiking boots.

And government officials like black-
backed jackals fight to line
their pockets, BMWs for some,
garbage cans for Katatura.

When a Himba man dies, where
are the dozens, the hundreds of cattle
skulls to honor his memory?

Rusting ships aground on the coast are
metaphors. Where are the potions

and salves? Where are the Nara melons?

The Healing Muse

The "Grateful" Series by Francis Musango

When someone has died, Francis said,
it is the custom to go to the mother and tell her.

Afternoon light fell on the worktable.
With the charcoal in his right hand, he had
six fingers. The charcoal made the sound
of slippers across a marble floor.

Why should I teach when thirty
of my fifty students are dead?

Light pooled under the easels: "Exodus,"
"Grateful 1." His brush was the sound of crickets
in dry grass and the men were roots
digging for what they could—an edge, a line.

At first in my village, when people died,
the family took time off from their jobs.

Christ hung in shadow on the south wall,
and the men grew faces in "Grateful 3."
They stretched out their arms and hands, fingers
jointed. *Now they do not take time.*

Now they are taking what they can
because they have nothing.

Charcoal made the sound of sand being swept
from the doorway. The women were singing
the song of firewood. The men were on
their way back. *On my way home,* Francis said,

I will stop to tell my niece's mother,
Your daughter is dead.

The Listening Eye

MARJORIE MANWARING

Letter from Zelda

My darling Scott, I feel so exploded
I can barely write, like a gourd
not knowing the hand that shakes me,

my mind a million seeds.
But weren't we once grand—a Ferris
wheel in Paris, spinning ourselves silly.

I never loved you more than when you bent
over your desk, pen gouging paper,
never hated you more—

your pen always blackening,
always my paper white as dogwood.
And though you cried,

Your relief heavied the air when you left me
in this room—where everything is cream-colored
rest—no silver shoes, dance floors, gin, or us.

I've planted a sunflower seed—I give it water
from the pitcher on my bedstand.
One day its yellow head will be as full as mine.

DMQ Review

Leaving Some Shell of Yourself

covered in sheets, you catch
your bus, pull the cord ten blocks
early, walk into the store that sells magic.

When your boss asks where you've been
you say you wanted to learn

how a thing disappeared comes back
how a velvet-lined cape
feels against skin.

Seattle/King County *Poetry on Buses* project

Answers from the Man Who Tried to Cook an Egg over the Eternal Flame in Paris

That flame burning for them
can't mask the stench

we shared. These days
of creak and recline my eyes

roll back to blood-
storms and soiled

fatigues. Edges
of calm breeding

practical jokes,
irreverence necessary

as K rations.
Boiling an egg

over The Flame,
I hear them whistling—

men I haven't touched
in fifty years. Cracking

smiles wide as the Arc,
belly-laughing, dog tags

jingling like a bell
choir. "Why not, doesn't

the fire belong to us?"
says Mac. Joey wants me to try

a sausage on a stick
or a can of SPAM and I think

about a discharge paper,
a finger, a hand.

Poets against the War web site and *Mirror Northwest*

Dhaulagiri Speaks

Nepal

Thunder roars and echoes down the gorge,
unraveling, shaking rain from the clouds

with a crack like timpani.
Gongs thick with lightning,
descend into our ears—
sizzling air.

Rain sprays off the rocks to meet the boulder-toothed
river, the rush
of air dense with sound,

a churning that leaves us
dizzy, that leaves us
like shivering wires

unsprung.

Making Music

Ubud, Bali

The light on the walls of this bamboo hut is rosy,
more luminous, as if it descends
from a foreign sun. It reminds me
of the blush of coral
blooming up from the rocky shore at Amed,
fragmenting slightly through the water
to my eye. So my body

feels altered, waved
by the ripples of tropical light.
The sounds rising from the village street
envelop me: hum of *bahasa indonesian*
like birds trilling; the clang and vibrato of gamelans
that murmur and enchant; the clop
of a cow's hooves on stones outside; the creak
and clap of rickshaw wheels.

I might be hovering mid-air
on clouds of sound. Or stepping out
to dance slowly with the gamelan dancers
in the *Mahabarrat*, my hands weaving
and limber like a crane's neck,
my body swirled in a sarong
like a rose bud.

I might be walking alone through the flutter of jungle
bamboo, skin collecting moisture,
the bird calls flamboyant and seductive,
drawing me on.

Oranges in Sunlight

Kathmandu, Nepal

And so the sun gives back
what it has taken.

The orange unleashes itself from the air,
from all surroundings.

It lies as gently as a pearl,
a drop of water.

So all beautiful entities
reside, present—to be consumed
by all our senses.
As gifts, they are willing
to be taken.
As infinite,

they are willing to remain.
My memory contains them,
and each one,
reacquainted,

cannot answer
to this first orange glimpse:
sunlight,

the fire radiance,
then touch, the porous skin,
the human,

and then the opening,
the orange spray rising—
like bathing in light.

Walt Whitman's War

Script: Craig McKenney
Pencils: Gervasio · Inks: Carlos Aón (Estudio Haus)

To Make Ends Meet

Near the ruined gate bound
with rope and wire, the wood's
weariness holds the shaggy pony
like a plea to settle.
The stone fence in the rough pasture
stops for this intersection, the leafless
scrub on its other side leans in a scramble
of sharp sticks sprinkled with berries.

When she walks here, she stops
with a pocketful of apple, her song
for the pony part chant, part cooing,
hand and apple to muzzle,
one hand to ruffle its scruffy mane.
She stops here missing Liam, stops
missing when its breath warms her hand,
when its turn turns to nuzzle.

Once her mother handed her a cup
and saucer so thin they settled in her hand
like a moth any wind might whisk away.
In the cup a dried spear thistle peeked
over the lip brittle and sharp as if her
first sip were steeped in prickly bracts
she needed to soothe with the cooling
whistle of her breath blown so.

She tells no one her fear of falling,
wants no one to know she's weightless,
walks in day the dream others have—
tumbling and no means to break their descent.

Once Liam asked why she watched her shadow
when she jumped, why she chased
the tufts of dandelions to make more wind.
She tried to answer, *Flying is not falling,*

shadows are tethers and ponies glide
only ten hands above solid ground.
Her mother knows. She gathers
things from her garden to fasten
the child, to help her with so much air.

ZYZZYVA

In Her Garden

After a good rain, goldfinch string
their music through the serviceberry trees.
My wife thinks she's Saint Francis.
She charms the cedar waxwing,
which lights close enough to touch.
She tells me Francis' theory of containers.
Take from the full, fill the empty.
This works for her, the music of birds,
a song from Francis, and all those nests
the shape of cupped hands waiting.

Metro Bus Poetry and *Everywhere Was Far*

The List of People You Wanted to Be

makes each slow day no one calls
a quiet to lie in like a hot bath.

Some days the simple nothingness
of your life is deep heat for the ache

envy worked into the muscle and tendon
you thought should be somebody.

The nobody you've begun to love
is calm in the halfway wisdom

common brings. The names you held
make a dream you drape in sparkling

ribbon, its shimmer all surface,
its hollow a barrel to echo laughter

at your naked want. Your list is a vest.
Those you've outgrown, snake out the fob

slinking to find a face fit for applause.
You find favor in failure. Fallen gods

make worship less than wishing. You flash
a gap-toothed grin at fame's mirage.

Faults are the path worn in stone steps.
You map veins trailing across your cheek,

follow the lines through your day, find
the way of a grandfather come to visit.

My Mother Poets

Would they have slapped my hands
and told me how the past is not worth
its weight in dirt? It is gold

if you lock it in a notebook
with a date and a match.
Would they tell me about the deaths

of their stolen husbands and children,
that grief was a luxury? Grief!
And What Ifs were for the wealthy—

not the swimming-in-gold rich,
but swimming-in-freedom wealthy,
so much freedom that these mothers would laugh

and cry, and hold me by my shoulders
until I could praise my past
with the brightness of this moment.

Telephone Job Interview

What's your dream job? She is after my head.
The recruiter's staccato invasion, a chilly hunter.

I turn to the window. Answers, the smart ones,
evade me. A weave of sailboats zigzags the lake.

Today, I have already communed with dreamers
who reach for the silver trunks of trees.

We sang with tears in our eyes. My body moans
to coil with an ex-lover, to read the Russians,

find myself safe in their vowels. What's your dream job?
On TV, cyclists pray with their shoulders, thighs peddle like windmills.

What's your dream job? Dream: eating licorice, naked.
Job: packing groceries, laundry, a day job. A blow job. Wait,

wait. Today, I have already sat with a young poet.
We wrote to Van Gogh, syllables on our cheeks.

What's your dream job? My mouth fills with apples. Hang up!
A chorus rises about red sheets and wrists. Write a poem!

Too many love poems, I say, too many love poems. The sailboats tip to
the wind, I am
living my dream and a cyclist crosses the finish line.

Villanelle

One night kindness brought me in for dinner,
fed my bony outline. I couldn't eat, I tried
to pray my way to hunger—but I'm only a beginner.

If hearts had hecklers, mine would call me sinner.
I can't endure the fights: I run, I hide and god I've lied—
but one night, a strange kindness bought me dinner

asked nothing of me, just to share a meal. It was winter.
I nodded, hid my teeth behind a toughened smile. Inside
I prayed for something witty: nothing—dumb beginner!

Not one line from Shakespeare, Donne, even Pindar
could I rescue from my memory—such mush! Too mired
down by kindness. So I panicked, left my dinner,

left my date with two desserts and me, again, the winner
of the only girl to chase down midnight tides.
I prayed the moon away, tonight, a fingernail beginner,

so quiet: I heard the truth undress more lies, a whimper
longing, climbing up my heels. It was cold and I was all lied
out. So I found kindness, gave my hands to him, not dinner—
we prayed for staying power, a patron saint for all beginners.

Kal

Bengali: "tomorrow" "yesterday"

In the study of my childhood home was a globe of the moon,
a muddied celadon, with the ancient magma oceans
just as they look from earth ... *Serenitiatis. Nubium.*
I'd turn the globe: ahead, back, swift,

slow. Would trace the fine blue scribbles that meant *height,*
made blunt mountains lap at the brims of basins. And wonder, then,
at how someone reasonable and smart
had marked lines of latitude and longitude—

fixed a lunar Orient, a West.
How the white fields and grey fields shaded and blanched

the face of the moon into cartoons of rabbit and man.
Years later I studied the moon's mantle and crust,

the colorless grit of spinel, feldspar. Looked
at photographs: an orange, I thought: newly peeled,

spoked with strings of pith. And looked closer still,
at the chemical signatures of comets, their glancing paths.
The ceaseless rain of meteor impacts.
And solar winds, raking grains of sand

into the moon's native soil. I read what
that polished globe spinning in my hand

—tomorrow/yesterday/tomorrow—
couldn't tell: a story of travelers and emigrants.

Story

My son and I
play catch on a brittle autumn night
beneath the shining porch light.

Three,
he shouts happily
every time he throws

up the ball: occluding the light,
erasing himself from my sight
until it falls to rest in my palms.

Simple props: rubber ball,
circle of light, a child
replete with joy.

We stage the story over and again:
how once we stood
waiting, separated

until a shadow in its arcing path
slipped, and revealed us,
each to each.

Summertime

Somewhere another mother, another summertime.
Starched sky, guests on the patio in short-sleeved shirts
and linen shifts. On a painted tray, mint juleps
crusted with ice. That is to say
I was there. I saw it with my own eyes:
Mother-doll. Father so good-looking
Miss Alice from down the street could not unpeel
her gaze all the night. The voices grew thick with drink
and in time their shadows spilled
down the brick and split at the rift
of stone and grass. How tenderly
he poured her drinks, as there the smiling mother sat.
Somewhere there is another mother, who rises
from the plastic chair, knocks the tumbler
out of his hand. Who steps over the sparkling glass,
across the deep green grass, all the way
to the dark, fruiting plum, who looks up at the child
weeping in the sky. *Hush, little baby.* How firm
her voice: *Don't you cry.*

Saint of Strays

St. What's-Your-Name, O patron saint of ur-
ban creatures (gray heads probing dumpsters left
ajar, thin whiskers poised for morning rain),
please bless this ragged beast asleep against
the door, the fishbone cartoon cat wrung out,
and Norway rat descended from the ships
left slumbering at the dock. St. Francis, when
he held his hands aloft, did he include
the common dove, the fly, the nest of new-
born shrews inside the wall? Is God the snap
of steel or poison dust that opens out
their veins to thin their blood, to drain the sweet
ripe raspberry-like hearts? O saint, forgive—
we who decide what creatures die, or live.

Imagine You Are the Last Child

Imagine you are the last child
at the end of the world,
after chatter and lecture

have drifted like motes,
unfinished sentences
settled among chairs.

Black rabbits,
wild and fearless,
thump patches of lawn.

Silence settles your throat
like milk in a worn cup.

*

Starlings chip
underbrush with their sharp feet.
Mice shiver in ivy.

You run through house
after house, turning on stereos,
ancient video machines:

Singing in the Rain
Lennon thrumming *Imagine*.
Frying pans, knives

clatter in a kitchen,
bacon and watermelon,
food for the end

of your flesh.

*

You find a pen—quill,
goose feather—and the letters,

a monk forming vowels,
inking nimbus and angel

in yolk and blood.

*

Wind washes your bones,
creeps under your shift,

wool thin as winter leaves.
Moon still mouths its full vowels,

the pond echoes the O of fish-
splash at evening, at nightfall.

No one to speak to, yet sounds
rise from your mouth.

*

Eat what you want.
Nothing left in the stores

but new apples rise green
on black branches,

eggs appear under errant
red hens.

Sleep as long as you care to,
words tapping dreams.

                    *

Maple seeds spin down
inside earth. You could go there,

give in, be happy.
Ducks slide into ponds.

                    *

Someone told you a story,
a boy and girl at the start of the world.

Fruit grew and their hearts filled up.
Talking came next, then something sad.

Then the story.

On Adam

Names hurt.
And not Zeus, not Medusa turns us
to sticks and stones—
there Ovid was joking. It was sculptures
he saw, bright Greek sculptures, cursed
in the gardens, now ruins.

Medusa indeed!
Do you think she painted
men, too, like an undertaker?
Did she name and play with her dolls,
rip off clothes, break their arms
or a nose?

Would a god turn men,
heart and soul, to foliage and stone
so they'd last? God-dance is riddance to bodies. It's man
who needs without end—dominion,
monument, and a name
to give a damn.
It's Adam.

The New Republic

Not a Blur

Close the bridges, stop conversations, the Angels
are practicing
  here—
    after the earthquake, during fires, out

of the drought blue. They roar through their perfect curve
wide open.
  Then *presto*—
    they're gone, startling day's dry eye

into applefall, and a bird into birthing, her shadow
large, her *wht—wht—wht*
    too low.
          On my shoe now, her out-of-the-blue egg shines

its yellow.

Most Wanted

Returns

I don't say farewells well.
Once I had the flu

and failed to be romantic.
Another time I left my coat behind,

so what looked like his change of heart
was a lesser return—to my absent mind.

Then I forgot to say good-bye—
he'd already left

so many times.
Believe me, I rehearse

these things for ages
afterwards.

Penumbra

The River's Dream

The Slaughter day fades into night & the Stuck
river's dream begins as a silver
shimmer. She is back to a time of red paint power that
reflects a less fearful state   the
outline
of
bare
trees
& a time before blackberries &
relentless settler prehension. Time of red paint power   end of
November when the harvest is in & her dreams are protected by miles
of
fog.

Letter Thirteen—Plum Stain

Poetry found in the sky
like giant Mars chasing the full ripe plum moon as if in
love—interstellar courting
is how bodies in the heavens demonstrate—
made gravity desirable again
in the August night sky above the Honda's pounding bass
a silent witness above the
bed in which dreams of hook shots & fast breaks are kept.
In the Slaughter sky
her makeup perfect this ripe plum full moon fallen plums
messed
up sidewalks all over town
sheets of falling unwanted fruit
the Russians learn about the Slaughter
sun
rises plums fall & Mars ran away w/ the moon.

Poetry—the desire to kiss eternity
lives to leave a ripe plum stain on the sidewalk of the future
in Slaughter where the
deep wounds open but don't reveal flesh deep
woods open reinvent themselves in an alder moment
                                        to show Slaughter the way.

Phrase taken from *On the Road to San Romano* by Andre Breton

Another Bird Song

May sun river reflection   a perceived bright silver angle w/ which the
chickadee sings his Thursday A.M. melody going
on bird nerve & the primitive hunger of sound.
The notion of sound as gift cottonwood down
downed in May on the ground under the dream head pillow so
Stuck in its insistence to follow its plan to mitigate this state we created. A
maple
tree a perch for early brunch surely this
throat
bobbing bird has a tender
vibrato & a word for Thursday but until Slaughter relents it's only
                                                nine cheerful notes.

Anagrammer

If you believe in the magic of language,
then *Elvis* really *lives*
and *Princess Diana* foretold *I end as car spin.*

If you believe the letters themselves
contain a power within them,
then you understand
what makes *outside tedious,*
how *desperation* becomes *a rope ends it.*

The circular logic that allows *senator* to become *treason,*
and *treason* to become *atoners.*

That *eleven plus two* is *twelve plus one,*
and an *admirer* is also *married.*

That if you could just rearrange things the right way
you'd find your true life,
the right path, the answer to your questions:
you'd understand how *the Titanic*
turns into *that ice tin,*
and *debit card* becomes *bad credit.*

How *listen* is the same as *silent,*
and not one letter separates *stained* from *sainted.*

Poetry

Missing *e*

Since you've been gone
I'm missing the *e*'s
that turn *rivers* into *reveries.*

Now *please* becomes *pleas,*
and my *emotions* are just *motions.*

I am trying to understand
the *lesson* in *one less.*

What makes an *antique quaint*
and *baudy* almost *beauty.*

Since you've been gone I'm missing
the *e* that makes *drama a dream,*
and *climax exclaim.*

I'm missing
the *e* that makes *breath*
breathe, and *last* not *least.*

Prairie Schooner

Turbidophilia

— love of trouble

Pleasure, ease, contentment: a bore.
Where's the rub? The snafu? The glorious glitch?
Tiff. Tizzy. Tumult. To-do. Remember:
no itch, no fuss: no pearls to string.
Feud, fit, flap, flurry.
Hoopla. Imbroglio. Rhubarb. Pickle.
What good's a shampoo without lather?
Soup unstirred? Wedding without a row?

I want spasm, spat, squabble, stink.
Brouhaha. Boondoggle. Conniption. Clash.
Calm's as good as dead: a plum-pit.
Give me ruckus, rowdydow, ruffle, snit.

Poetry

The Exile Reconsiders

for Ubax

Tonight, the tides pull through your shoulders,
take up residence in between
your breasts, the teeth of the pocket comb.

Stars shoot themselves
along the edges of each year
and the night's purple darkness

finds you; refuses to go.

How to parse a palimpsest life?
The seasons

of paperwork traveling
like a magician's fist
disappearing one country for the next.

A legend of broken maps
in your bones

pale blue aerogramme by the phone.

Your grandmother's cattle,
rhythmic dots in the fields,
leave a trail of milk on the tongue.

Tomorrow, the hoopoe inside you

will rise up
call above the seaboard—
cool mistress of turn and return;

mist-lit, two-fold, you leave
or linger here,
undiminished.

Cures Include Travel

Scriptorium

No ink from crushed oak or smarting apples,
no swan feather quills, no Ogham stone,

just a woman of the notebook with her vision
fine pen taking up residence alone.

One long and narrow window seat, three chairs
a desk, a stove, answer most her needs

as she answers the page with consonants, holds
the vowels' open-hearted pleas.

As the night continues on, counted out
in cups of tea, will she conceive or miscarry?

In the hard light of morning will the pigments ignite,
the words intermarry: gold leafed, extraordinary?

Cures Include Travel

To My Mother, Dead Eight Years

When I travel out of country
you can't follow as easily, can't click
your tongue around my thighs'
circumference, can't chart my unsocial
social life. I've flown Cape Town
to Jerusalem fleeing condemnation
yet, our cold words cling like the dying
roots of old pot-bound plants: cracked, unforgiven.

But that's just half the days, half
the lines inside my head. I've kept
the way you welcomed each guest:
candles lit at dusk on Friday evenings,
sweet fruit and chilled ginger ale. *Never
hate anyone* you said, but couldn't hold to.
And if there was little love to spare
we had crisp sheets, clean underwear.

Cures Include Travel

Fukuoka says

A small man with fly-away white hair,
Masanobu Fukuoka lives in a tiny hut
surrounded by citrus trees. Each spring

and fall since the Great War forty years
ago he sows barley, rice, rye, then retires
to lie content on his hillside in one of

three kimono he still owns. Nature is
perfect, Fukuoka says, human knowledge
is meaningless. Become a foolish man, then

you can understand, see what must not
be done. Fukuoka-san says there is
one last chance to save the world—

we must take over the bombers, throw away
our implements of war, pack the missiles
with seeds of vegetables, fruit trees

and grain, shoot them up into the ozone.
Spread seeds over all the earth. Scatter them
in the deserts. Cover the green

imitation pastures and concrete lawns
with seeds. When the rains come,
the world will once more be a jungle.

In the second year each plant will choose
its own best place, and in the third year
small animals will increase, worms beget

worms, their generations breaking the
rubble of superhighways and shopping malls,
and the earth will be green again.

Fukuoka says we are holding tight to the tail
of a plow horse running fast away from Eden,
no time left for anything now, only sowing

seed, spreading straw. When there is enough
food for every man, woman, child, bellies
everywhere filled with the fruits growing

closest to their hoes and hands, people won't
be so uneasy, Fukuoka says. First fix
this ailing Earth, *Then* there can be peace.

Mr. Cogito, Poets at the Faire and *Saxifrage*

Yahrzeit

Ten years after your death
I still long to hold you—

a teaspoon of ashes
whirled away from me
light as breath.

Little daughter,
so many loves are cut off
by desire and pain,

yet this memory persists
like a phantom limb:

the brief candle of your life,
blue as forget-me-not.

Arcturus

The Orange

The rabbi refuses tea from my Belgian grandmother's cup,
accepts instead into his narrow, long-fingered hand
a perfect miniature sun. It glows in the room's dim light.

He passes it between his nose and his dusty beard, breathes in
its fragrance like that of a fine cigar. He closes his eyes, says,
"Next year in Jerusalem." I wonder if he believes this,

yet can see with his tender eye the desert blossoming
with orange trees; Ezekiel's wheel going down in flames
behind the walled city his people have never quite possessed.

At the exact angle prescribed by the Law that determines whose
cups he may drink from, what fruits he may peel, the precise distance
the door to the street must be left open while he speaks with a woman

he must not touch even to say goodbye, he plunges the black-rimmed
nail of his opposing thumb into the bright surface, sends galaxies
of citrus oil——each molecule a sun——spraying out

in a pungent mist. It hovers in the cool air of my all-too-sanguine house
like the dizzying white perfume of the night-blooming cereus.
"God is good," he observes as if surprised each time, licks the juice

running toward the cuff of his ancient, ill-fitting coat,
then begins the long peel he is sure will reveal all mysteries——
God's immutable Law, source of all sweetness not segmented, but whole.

The Written ARTS and www.poetrymagazine.com

MICHAEL SPENCE

The Last Stop in Golden Gardens

As I reach it, I park the bus.
On my left a vacant lot
Too shallow to hold a house
Let me look for years
Out across the bay
To the Olympics. They rasp
The sky with their jagged line.
But the peaks that matter
In this age are those on graphs,
Marking the altitudes of money.
A blueprint saw the land
Wasn't big enough: more
Was trucked in. Like a forest
Made square, two stories
Of beams and rafters rise—
As if the final end of want
Is to make beauty private.
I want to hate the workers,
But they're just young men:
When they see me watching,
They wave. They're nailing
And planing the walls of a box—
A camera that over and over
Will take the same picture,
Its owner keeping his view
By staying in the dark. Starting
The engine, I wave goodbye.

The New York Quarterly

Addendum to the Safety Officer's Account

When the spanwire
Snapped like a line mooring Seaman Holt
To this world, the severing released a flood
Of paper from his body. I had to fill
Every sheet with words.
A month washed by—
I'd written the letter to his family,
The accident report, the memoranda
To the various departments that had fed
And clothed and paid him, my journal entry.
His face began to lose its puzzled look,
Dissolving in the darkness of my thoughts.

The Shore Patrol had fished him out of bars,
Disorderly and drunk; he'd been written up
For ragged dungarees, skipping watch
On the quarterdeck and unrep duties
On fueling details. His final day, though,
He was on that rig.
And then Personnel
Called for a Terminal Evaluation.
In every category on that form—
Skills, discipline, personal appearance—
I wrote a 4.0. The yeoman typed
From this a "smooth eval" which I proofread:
The comma at its end I whited out
To a period.

The New Republic

Father Gathers his Breath

In the early dark,
I'd wake—those mornings, before you shaved
To leave for work, you'd come in
And kiss me goodbye. Moonlight
Washed the room the palest blue
As though it were underwater. Your whiskers felt
Like small needles;
Five years old, sometimes I'd lie still,
Pretending to be asleep.
You'd blow gently on my face, and wait
For my eyes to open.

The unseen light
Of x-rays found the spots of light growing
Quietly in your lungs. Your last year,
You went back to the Florida beach
Where you swam when young.
Your short, clipped strokes
Fought the water, not letting it touch
Your face. Home again, you hammered
The flight of stairs you'd put off fixing—
Each *whack!* like a gunshot—and sanded the rail
Smooth as your shaven jaw.

You died at home in August,
A blue moon about to rise. When mother called,
You lay on your couch, your breath rapid
Like a diver getting ready
To enter the sea. I think you hung on,
Waiting for me, so she wouldn't be alone.
Kneeling beside you, I called

Your name, but you had begun the arc.
I watched your eyes close. Your whiskers
Prickled my lips. I stopped myself
From blowing on your face.

The North American Review

Talking Thai, White Center, Seattle

At HengHeng Market, I look for Thai faces
among Maori, Hispanic, Vietnamese, Korean.
I sort tones from syllables: Chinese,
Mextex, Spanglish, HipHop, Hmong, Chechan.

My new kin, all Thai, call me *Ya* (Grandma)
and I shop here, bagging up bumpy limes,
hoping they are the *ma groud* listed
in the recipes in my new cookbook.

Grandmothers dressed in home clothes—
woven and hand knotted—
pick through trays of peppers, fingers
catching firm ones, shiny ones, hot ones.

Dichan mii look chai song kha
(I have two sons), I tell the old ladies'
daughters who, dressed in cotton sportswear,
stand back, carrying their mothers' full bags.

I ask *Hew kao mai kha?* (Are you hungry?)
of grown sons who hold their mothers' elbows
as the old women falter, bending
to the close work of choosing catfish.

Penyanra kriang look chai pben Thai kha
(My son's wife is Thai), I tell slack teens
ushering grandma around. They are tall,
t-shirts emblazoned with "America sucks."

I am too young, too straight, too restless
to be a grandmother, but I want to learn
to purse my lips and smile at the same time
to say correctly blood's spice: *gleua* (salt).

How We Love

Here where we women fall in love with old men,
we stand in their gravel driveways,
taking home their blackberry jam,
slow conversations about the practical,
carving meaning into the late afternoons.
When we drive off, they think about us,
re-sort the small, medium and large ratchets,

take the rototiller out for one more turn,
feel pain flurry through their secret bodies,
they who had no children and no loves
to scent their sparky days and achy dawns.
Where are the old dogs they feed?

And now we women who fell in love
again phone around, gather poems and pies,
fluff the bouquets up front—dahlias,
vine maple, crab apple, sunflowers,
anything orangy, autumnly, homegrown—
and get the midday together
to come down the driveway once again,
and grind our teeth, saying how
we hate it when the good ones do that,
how they step outside in the moon night,
how one by one they leave us, how they die.

Eating Only

Eating only dime-sized clams,
the aunties sit on the deck.

With their fingers, they detach
each plump body,
mantle and siphon,
guts full of seaweed bloom.

The auntie whose time has come
finds a minute crab,
white, commensal,
in the fold of the clam flesh.

The other aunties toast her luck.
They share a beer. They talk.

Tide Turn

Cantos a los Orishas #1

for C.S.

Purple sunset drives its wedge
across my skull anterior,
I, cross-eyed with pain
from its bilingual shaft.
On one side is writ a prayer,
Sanskrit text weeping the death of slaves.
On the other—Mother of God!—
the same tale told in the tongue of Yoruba.
And here, sharp incisors have bitten
punctuation into the splintered wedge.

Behind my eyeballs, clavé throbs.
Beyond the sunset black
overcomes the purple benediction.
An apparition raises its voice,
What lies beyond my death throes?
And what of north winds blown from my mouth?
Or the westerly Chinook that warmed
my brothers' bones?

Great aunt in her rocker,
cross-armed,
hums gospel hymns.
Child chants learned on Sunday afternoons
spill from elder lips.

I turn the last page,
sing one final verse.
A quarter note weeps a tear.
My body, soul's slave, wilts,
a minor key teething,

I am lost,
my youth, a diminished chord;
a big band salsas and I can no longer dance.

Obatalá! Elegguá! Ogún!
I offer incense, cigars,
spit rum to the four corners.
I am a man,
a purple shaft of pain,
scholar of art and sound.

Oshún,
yellow my lips
with your honey,
the bite of rum.
Spit me,
sing me,
candle my altar.
Drink me
my mother's honey.

Capistrano

In France, I'm told,
if a swallow falls from the sky,
legs too short
for wings' longing flight,
one must lift it in cloth hands
like this year's crow
fallen from first glide.

For two days under hovering caws
that warned you away,
you lifted and tossed the young crow,
fed it worms,
worried over scent-tainted wings.
Then one day its fledgling flight held the air.
I have slept above the touch of ground,
taken insects on wing with eyes sonar sharp.
You and I have mated on currents of air.
In our passion I fell, your scent on my wings.
My legs grew short,
I flapped for loft, mute air denied me.

Gather me in cloth and toss.
In a stream of wind I will leap on sleek wings.
Your cords of light bind and release me,
release and bind me.
With mud and saliva,
again and again
I nest in your mission eaves.

Chrysanthemum

Songcatcher

She whistles on wicker legs,
winged archaic wishbones,
her naked gold eye,
a raptor with song in her teeth.
She lights in your mind,
a cave pictographed
with rust horses, boar and wild ox.
She feasts the meat of hollows,
soars the downbeat
improv of stalactites.
Drip!
The prick of moisture!

She hunts—
nails click when they land.
You offer her calf
skin offer to wrap her in your fore
skin She offers you
the hide off her feet,
the dangerous red slit
where her seams part.

She sings two
notes You sing three
notes She sings papyrus
between her legs
notations keeping score
of flute and drum,
the flit of gnat and note
dense ass blue,
breath
the weight of a sigh.

In her claws your kid
skin Havana red
streaks on albino
skin where her nails
drip your blood,
her score regurged in your hands.

The Comstock Review

St. Mary of Egypt

Skin circles her like bark
clinging to dead twigs.
Once her moon-colored arms
smelled of the recent flowers
frequented by bees. Now
white hair collects light
from Venus until dawn grows again.

That was how Jeremiah first saw her.
He was out, as was his habit,
listening for voices that drifted
between shadows in the sand.
At one time he had been such a voice.

It was her hair. As it drew in
the night of the desert
it looked metallic, icy.
When he touched it his hand met
something dense and resinous.
It had been some time since
he had spoken. But Jeremiah
still understood little of silence
as this woman appeared,
a dry branch that might shrink
into the cold night. He knew
they needed to talk.

A desert creature, she hid
during midday. He followed her,
speaking of the past, something
she rarely mentioned.
Her life was devoted to listening
for God's feral song, a song

that never changed
whether she heard it scorched
by the sun of early afternoon
or any phase of the moon,
even in the back of her cave
waiting for the runoff to abate
after a spring shower.

Her mind and heart bloom as once
her desiccated skin had and might now
if water was poured over her.
Walking out of her tattered clothes,
eyes endless as the firmament,
she hands him bread, motions
to a full jar of water, and says
"Tell me what you know about love."

Monkscript

Evensong on the North Bank

The sun has not yet set but the air
is seriously cooler, carried by a breeze

from the west, a breeze that
was not here a few minutes ago,

a breeze that ends the nine-note song
of the white-crowned sparrow.

Mallards, gulls and geese floating
in the water are silent as are the cormorants

gathering in the poplars on the south bank.
A robin chirps from trees somewhere

behind me, the same trees
sprinkled earlier by voices of bushtits.

Eastbound, two young men steer
a wolf-colored outboard into view.

For a moment they turn left, aiming
in the direction of the goose,

then veer back on course
leaving the goose floating

next to their wake
like they had never been there.

From the trees the cloud of a low
harmonic falls around me like a piece

of silk. Above, eleven cormorants
roost. More arrive as I watch, filling

the tree with a communal sound
like the crackling of a blow-burning fire.

Settled now, the glowing embers of their voices
join in vespers, notes from a scale only they can sing.

Biographies

ELIZABETH AUSTEN was the WPA/WSAC/Humanities Washington "road show poet" for 2007, bringing poetry to underserved rural areas in Washington State. Each Monday at 2:00 p.m. on "The Beat" on KUOW public radio, she provides commentary on Pacific Northwest poetry readings, and she teaches throughout the state. Her audio CD, *skin prayers*, is available at elizabethausten.org.

DEBORAH BACHARACH's work has appeared in *Calyx, Many Mountains Moving, Blue Mesa Review,* and others. She is a freelance writer and editor living in Seattle.

JANÉE J. BAUGHER's "Coördinates of Yes" was a semifinalist for the *Tupelo* First Book Prize and is available through interlibrary loan. *The Body's Physics* was a semifinalist for the Saturnalia Books Poetry Prize and a finalist for the Ontario Prize. She teaches at Interlochen Center for the Arts each summer.

ALLEN BRADEN has received fellowships from the National Endowment for the Arts and Artist Trust. His work is published in *The New Republic, Virginia Quarterly Review, The Southern Review, Threepenny Review, Georgia Review, Best New Poets 2005,* and elsewhere. He teaches creative writing and interdisciplinary composition at Tacoma Community College.

PATRICIA CURRAN served six years on the Washington State Arts Commission, chairing the Arts in Education Program. She lives in Kent with her husband, Pete. She's published in *Seattle Review, Poetry Seattle, The Written Arts, West Wind Review, Arnazella,* and *Poultry, A Magazine of Voice.* Her chapbook is titled *Bird Babies.* She is treasurer of The Northwest Renaissance.

PHYLLIS COLLIER's poetry book, *Cain's Daughters,* was published by Blue Unicorn Press. Her poems, essays, and reviews appear in many literary and popular magazines, and she worked at Boeing, Microsoft, and North Seattle Community College. She received awards from

National Endowment for the Arts, Nimrod Pablo Neruda, National Writers Union, and Willow Springs, and received a Ragdale Foundation residency.

ALICE DERRY's most recent volume of poetry is *Strangers To Their Courage* (Louisiana State University Press, 2001). She has also published *Stages of Twilight, Clearwater* (Blue Begonia Press), and a chapbook of translations from Rainer Rilke. A finalist for the Washington Book Award, she teaches English and German at Peninsula College where she co-directs the Foothills Writers' Series.

DONNA FRISK received an MFA from Antioch University-Los Angeles and published in magazines such as *Synapse Magazine, PoetsWest Literary Journal,* and *Pontoon 3.* A former personnel manager, she was interested in how we process visual and other sensory information and "how a word or words on a page can create the same physiological response in the reader as actual sense data." She died unexpectedly in 2007.

PENNY GERKING facilitates writing groups at her local library and runs an on-line fiction forum. Her poetry has appeared in print journals and e-zines, and she is working on a young adult novel.

PESHA JOYCE GERTLER was Seattle's Poet Populist from 2005-2006 and is founder and coordinator of the long-running After Long Silence reading series. Her poems have appeared in the *Calyx, Poems for Peace Project Anthology, Bridges: A Journal for Jewish Feminists and Their Friends,* and others. Her poem "Ballad of A Welfare Mother" was featured in singer Linda Allen's Women's History Album, *Mama Wanted To Be A Rainbow Dancer.*

ALLISON GREEN is a novelist and poet. Her novel, *Half-Moon Scar,* was published by St. Martin's Press. She teaches at Highline Community College, where she is chair of the Arts and Humanities Division, and at Richard Hugo House in Seattle.

JOSEPH GREEN's poems have been published throughout the United States, as well as in Ireland and Germany, and have been collected in *His*

Inadequate Vocabulary (1986), *Deluxe Motel* (1991), *Greatest Hits: 1975-2000*, and *The End of Forgiveness*, which won the Floating Bridge Press Poetry Chapbook Award for 2001. He was PEN Northwest's Margery Davis Boyden Wilderness Writer and a resident at the Dutch Henry Homestead and at Fundacion Valparaiso in Mojacar, Spain.

SAMUEL GREEN is Washington State's first Poet Laureate. His tenth collection of poetry, *The Grace of Necessity*, has been published by Carnegie Mellon University Press and received the 2008 Washington State Book Award for poetry. His other books and chapbooks include *Working in the Dark* (Grey Spider Press) and *Vertebrae* (Eastern Washington University Press). He is Distinguished Northwest Writer in Residence at Seattle University. He has also taught at Southern Utah University, Western Wyoming Community College, and in countless public schools. A Highline Community College graduate, he is the 2008 Alumnus of the Year. Sam and his wife Sally co-edit the award-winning Brooding Heron Press.

MARIA GROAT collaborated with poet Robert Hasselblad for the Visual Verse project sponsored by the Contemporary QuiltArt Association. Her award-winning art quilts have been shown nationally and internationally and are in several collections. She currently resides on Bainbridge Island.

ROBERT HASSELBLAD lives and writes in Tacoma. His poetry has appeared most recently in *StringTown*, *Lynx Eye*, *Heeltap*, and *New Song*. His poem sequence "Word Salad" was featured, with quilt art by Maria Groat, in Visual Verse, an art show exhibiting collaborative work between U.S. poets and Northwest textile artists.

SHARON HASHIMOTO's poems have appeared in *The American Scholar*, *Bamboo Ridge*, *Crab Orchard Review*, *Poetry*, *The Seattle Review*, and others. Her full-length book of poetry is *The Crane Wife*. She also has had short stories published in *North American Review*, *Crab Orchard Review*, *Seattle Magazine*, and others. She teaches at Highline Community College.

HOLLY J. HUGHES' chapbook, *Boxing the Compass*, won the 2007 Floating Bridge chapbook contest. Her poems have appeared in a number of anthologies, most recently *Dancing with Joy: 99 Poems*. She's spent twenty-five summers working on boats in Alaska and winters teaching writing at Edmonds Community College. She lives in a log cabin built in the 1930s in Indianola.

TOM C. HUNLEY is an assistant professor of English at Western Kentucky University. His latest books are *Teaching Poetry Writing: A Five Canon Approach* (Multilingual Matters LTD. 2007), *Octopus* (Logan House Press 2008), and *The Tongue* (Wind Publications 2004). He is a Highline Community College alumnus.

CHRISTOPHER J. JARMICK is co-author of the suspense thriller *The Glass Cocoon* and has published articles, interviews, short stories, and poems in *Cambridge Book Review*, *Real Change*, and *Pontoon 7*. He's president of PEN Washington and board member of PEN-USA and The Washington Poets Association. In the past he made documentaries for PBS; he now works as a financial advisor.

LONNY KANEKO is a poet, playwright and fiction writer and was a prizewinner in the Coeur d'Alene Festival of Arts poetry contest, *Amerasia Journal's* short story contest, and received the Pacific Northwest Writers Conference award and a National Endowment for the Arts fellowship. Incarcerated in Minidoka, Idaho, where he spent his preschool years, he is working on new poems about the camps. His chapbook of poetry *Coming Home from Camp* reflects his family's experiences. He teaches at Highline Community College and lives on Vashon Island.

SUSAN LANDGRAF's work has appeared in more than 150 publications in the United States and abroad. Nominated twice for the Pushcart Prize and featured on KUOW's Sound Focus, she's received Jack Straw, Academy of American Poets, Fulbright-Hays, and National Endowment for the Humanities grants and a Theodore Morrison Scholar in Poetry award. Susan recently had a chapbook accepted for publication. She teaches at Highline Community College.

MARJORIE MANWARING, a freelance writer and editor, has taught poetry writing to children and adults and is an associate editor for the online poetry journal the *DMQ Review*. Her poems have appeared in *The Seattle Review*, *5 AM*, *Sentence*, *Karamu*, *Pontoon*, and other journals. She was a semi-finalist in the 2005 "Discover"/*The Nation* contest.

JILL MCGRATH, a poet, teacher, and freelance editor, has a chapbook *The Rune of Salt Air* and has been published in *The Seattle Review*, *The MacGuffin*, *Southern Poetry Review*, *West Wind Review*, and *Poet & Critic*, among others. She has a manuscript about her two-year journey in Asia on a tandem bicycle and about work she did on tourism magazines in Nepal.

CRAIG MCKENNEY says that in an age where technology (text messaging, blogging, word processing/graphic design software, website design) has continued to transform the way we think about text, we must embrace the visuals that can help us produce our texts. He was awarded the Xeric Grant for Comic Book Self-Publishing for Part 1 of his graphic novel, *The Brontes: Infernal Angria* (illustrated by Rick Geary). A writer of comics, he teaches at Highline.

KEVIN MILLER has published two collections of poems: *Light That Whispers Morning*, winner of the Bumbershoot Weyerhaeuser Publication Award, and *Everywhere Was Far*, both by Blue Begonia Press. He received an Artist's Trust grant and has been a member of the Jack Straw Writers Group. He has worked in public education in Washington State for thirty-four years and was a Fulbright Exchange teacher in Denmark.

TATYANA MISHEL teaches workshops and coaches writers through Write Now!, which emphasizes surprise and risk, as well as keeping the creative muscle in shape. Her poems and interviews have been published in *Cranky Literary Journal*, *4th Street*, and others. A former editor of *Elle* magazine, she currently writes book features for the *Seattle P.I.*

SATI MOOKHERGEE received an Artist Trust GAP (Grants for Artist Projects) Award and an Artist Trust/Washington State Arts Commission Fellowship Award. She was a nominee for the Pushcart Prize in 2000 and 2001 and a semifinalist in *The Nation/Discovery* Poetry Contest in 2002. She received a degree in Medicine from the University of Washington School of Medicine in 1998 and most recently has been active in electing the new mayor of Bellingham.

ARLENE NAGANAWA, a teacher since 1973, has been published in *Diner; Crab Orchard Review; 88: A Journal of Contemporary American Poetry; New Delta Review; Cider Press Review; The Seattle Review; Mid-American Review; Caketrain; Crab Creek Review;* and *The Forbidden Stitch, An Asian American Women's Anthology* (Calyx). She was awarded two Seattle Arts Commission grants and nominated for a Pushcart Prize in 2005.

MURIEL NELSON has a full-length collection of poems, *Part Song* (Bear Star Press, 1999), and a chapbook, *Most Wanted* (ByLine Press, 2003) and has appeared in *88: A Journal of Contemporary American Poetry, The National Poetry Review, The New Republic, Ploughshares, The Prague Post, Snake Nation Review,* and others. Nominated twice for the Pushcart Prize, she holds master's degrees from the Warren Wilson MFA Program and University of Illinois School of Music.

PAUL E. NELSON co-founded SPLAB in Auburn and holds an M.A. in *Organic Poetry.* He's been published around the world in *Dirt, The Argotist, Fulcrum,* and *Olson Now,* and has interviewed Allen Ginsberg, Anne Waldman, Michael McClure, and others. The work that appears in this anthology is from his epic *A Time Before Slaughter.*

PETER PEREIRA is a family physician in Seattle and was a founding editor of Floating Bridge Press. His books include *Twin* (Grey Spider 2000) and *Saying the World* (Copper Canyon 2003), which won the Hayden Carruth Award and was a finalist for the Lambda Literary Award, the Triangle Publishing Award, and the PEN USA Award in Poetry. *What's Written on the Body* was released by Copper Canyon Press in 2007. His poems appear in *Poetry, Prairie Schooner, New England*

Review, and *Journal of the American Medical Association.* He presents on Poetry & Medicine at medical schools and writing conferences across the country.

SUSAN RICH is author of *The Cartographer's Tongue,* winner of the PEN USA and Peace Corps Awards for poetry, and a second collection, *Cures Include Travel,* by White Pine Press. She has been awarded an Artist Trust Fellowship and a GAP grant. Recent poems appear in *Alaska Quarterly Review, Bellevue Literary Review, Quarterly West,* and *Witness.*

MARJORIE ROMMEL lives in Auburn, Washington, six blocks from where she was born. A reporter and editor, her fiction, nonfiction, and poetry have appeared in more than 100 publications, including *The Seattle Times, The Christian Science Monitor, Monitor Radio, View Northwest Magazine, Washington Magazine, Organic Gardening, My Weekly (London), Signal International, Vagabond, Dark Orchid,* and others. She was a Willard R. Espy Literary Foundation resident in 2000.

MICHAEL SPENCE has driven public transit buses in the Seattle area for more than twenty years. His poems have appeared in *The New Republic, The New Criterion, The North American Review, The Sewanee Review, The Yale Review,* and others. He has published three books of poetry; his latest is *Adam Chooses* (Rose Alley Press). He is a 2008 Jack Straw award recipient.

ANN SPIERS' *Long Climb into Grace* is the latest in Foothills Publishing's Poets on Peace Series. Her chapbooks are *Tide Turn, Volcano Blue,* and *Herodotus Poems.* Published in *Calyx, Fine Madness, Beloit Poetry Review, Crab Creek Review,* and others, she serves as newsletter editor for the Audubon Society and coordinates conservation projects. She co-founded *The Seattle Review* and co-produced and hosted a poetry show on KRAB radio.

M. ANNE SWEET, a poet and artist, has published a poetry collection titled *Nailed to the Sky* from Gazoobi Tales Publishing. Her work has appeared in *The Comstock Review, Crab Creek Review, Raven Chronicles,*

Pontoon, Main Street Rag, and others. She won the Bart Baxter Poetry in Performance Award and works on poetry-music collaborations. She's had one-person shows of her visual art in Seattle and Federal Way.

DIANE WESTERGAARD received a GAP grant and was part of the Jack Straw Writer's Program. Her work has appeared in *Three Rivers Poetry Journal, Bainbridge Island Poets and Artists Calendar, Kansas Quarterly, Prairie Schooner, Bayou,* and others. With guitarist Garylee Johnson, she co-produced and co-wrote *Ghost in the Garden,* a chapbook and audiotape.